CW00417359

The Right Genes

Nick Hamilton

2QT (Publishing) Ltd

First Edition published 2022 by
2QT Limited (Publishing)
Settle, N. Yorkshire

Copyright © Nick Hamilton

The right of Nick Hamilton to be identified as the author of
this work has been asserted by him in accordance with the
Copyright, Designs and Patents Act 1988

All rights reserved. This book is sold subject to the
condition that no part of this book is to be reproduced, in
any shape or form. Or by way of trade, stored in a retrieval
system or transmitted in any form or by any means,
electronic, mechanical, photocopying, recording, be lent,
re-sold, hired out or otherwise circulated in any form of
binding or cover other than that in which it is published
and without a similar condition, including this condition
being imposed on the subsequent purchaser, without prior
permission of the copyright holder.

Publisher Disclaimer:
The events in this memoir are described according to the
author's recollection; recognition and understanding of
the events and individuals mentioned and are in no way
intended to mislead or offend. As such the Publisher does
not hold any responsibility for any inaccuracies or opinions
expressed by the author. Every effort has been made to
acknowledge and gain any permission from organisations
and persons mentioned in this book. Any enquiries should
be directed to the author.

Cover image: © Radio Times/Immediate Media

Printed by IngramSpark

A CIP catalogue record for this book is available
from the British Library

ISBN 978-1-914083-42-6

For Helen
Who was and continues to be my inspiration.

Preface

This is a story about the relationship between a son and his dad and how, from the off, it was obvious that the son would turn out to be a 'chip off the old block'. The individual stories are as close to fact as I can remember, which makes it a 'semi-factual' story. In reality it is irrelevant that I was also the son of the most popular television gardener there's ever been!

I once read that the middle child is more likely to be the one most like their father. I'm not sure if this was written by an eminent psychologist or it's an urban myth, but with me I think it hits the nail on the head.

During the seventeen years my dad appeared at 8.30pm each Friday evening on BBC Two's *Gardeners' World*, he was watched by millions of people. Most were avid gardeners looking for their gardening fix to prepare them for a full weekend in the garden or on the allotment, but there was also a significant number of husbands, wives, partners and children who watched – often because the household only had one television. Children watched as it was better than doing homework or household chores, as was often the case for the partners of avid gardeners who wanted to avoid doing the washing-up! However, there were many non-gardeners who watched Dad on *Gardeners' World* because they enjoyed the programme even though they didn't garden. He had a captivating, natural way about him and viewers really took to his presenting style.

Dad followed the likes of Percy Thrower, Peter Seabrook, Clay Jones, Arthur Billet and Geoffrey Smith. They were all traditional gardeners who appeared in shirts and ties, having removed their jackets prior to getting stuck in. Then this bloke in jeans and a checked shirt appeared in the late 1970s – and, God forbid, his top button was undone! He was like a breath of fresh air and it was clear that viewers were absolutely ready for this change.

During the time he presented *Gardeners' World*, these millions of viewers got to know him inside out. Or at least they thought they did.

In order to know the man behind the camera, the private Geoff Hamilton, you need to know not only his background but how his life, work, family, and particularly his children, moulded him as a person. The best way for me to help you do that is to write about my life with my soon-to-be-famous Dad. This was an idea I had for a while. It was my wife Helen who encouraged me to put fingers to keyboard and set all my stories down on paper, otherwise the idea might still be rattling around in my head.

The first draft of this book was written while I was

sitting with Helen in Peterborough City Hospital Oncology Department as she underwent chemotherapy treatment. That may seem odd for a book that is full of humour, but it's not if you know me, Helen or my dad. Odd is very much what we did!

I've really enjoyed putting into words the first of my two-book series. Whether you were aware of my dad or not, I hope this story makes you smile.

Chapter One

It really was never going to be particularly difficult because she'd done it all before. All it needed was a tensing of the stomach muscles, a squeeze of her buttocks and he was out!

It was the 15th of August 1936, a clear, warm, star-studded night, pretty average for the time of year, when Geoffrey Stephen Ham was born a mere two minutes before his twin, Anthony. To his parents, Rose and Cyril Ham, it was an uneventful birth but, most importantly for Geoffrey, he emerged the older twin, a position he would exploit for the rest of his life. The only glitch was that he was not the oldest son, merely the middle one. Barry, born three years previously, was waiting to greet his new siblings.

Those present at the birth were not aware that Rose had just given birth to a star as bright as those in the night sky, one that would enlighten, enhance and improve the lives of millions of people. Rose didn't realise at the time that she'd had a narrow escape; as Geoffrey would become the greatest television gardener of his generation, he could – and should – have emerged clutching his spade!

This recently expanded family lived in a small three-bedroomed terrace house with a yard in the East End of London. They shared the house with Rose's parents, Harriet and Alfred Graham, but with two new additions to the Ham family the house was now becoming very cramped.

Rose had aspired to greater things for some time. She longed to leave the dark, dismal and unhealthy East End and take her husband and three boys to a greener, leafier life; in the process, she could elevate their social standing. Those who knew Rose were clear that social standing was more important to her than greenery. This was the utopian lifestyle she had dreamt of as a teenager.

It had always been Rose's dream, because Cyril was not a willing partner in her vision. He was East End through and through, a bit of a wheeler-dealer, and his life plan was simple: to stay where they were with the life they had. He definitely wasn't a countryside sort of person. However, he knew the writing was on the wall and he had no option but to go along wherever that fairy tale took them. Rose had the stronger will and determination, a will and determination only matched by her mother's, so ultimately she called the shots in the Ham family.

Rose knew she couldn't push through this life change on her own. Extricating yourself from such an environment didn't happen often, so she needed her husband's help. But Cyril had always been popular within this community; he had many, many friends and associates, although Rose despised this close-knit East End 'family'. She wanted more and she wanted better. She didn't fit in with his friends any more but, as fate would have it, it was Cyril's network of friends that set Rose and the family on the road to her idea of a better life.

Eighteen months before the start of World War Two, to Rose's surprise one of Cyril's closest friends came good. Through the vast web of the East End network, he had heard of the perfect property. He passed this information, scribbled on the back of an empty Woodbine cigarette packet, to his good friend. Deep down Cyril was gutted, but he knew what this would mean to his wife so he went home and gave Rose the life-changing news she yearned for: there was a rather lovely semi-detached house in Broxbourne, Hertfordshire. The only fly in the ointment was that it was on the market for a whopping £400! It would take a lifetime to pay it off but this was Rose's dream move and earned Cyril at least a week's worth of brownie points.

Young Geoffrey was only two years old when the family drove out of the murky East End towards their new life in Hertfordshire. As they turned onto the Mile End Road, he didn't notice the dull, sooty colours of the roadside trees because they were normal to him. As they forged onwards through North London, the number of trees seemed to multiply faster than the miles per hour on their speedometer. The green, chlorophyll-filled leaves started to shine through and Geoff's young eyes saw colours they had not witnessed before. This was a seminal moment for Geoffrey; not only was his whole life being uprooted but also he was being introduced to nature for the first time. The seed had been sown.

Crossing into Hertfordshire was a bittersweet moment for Cyril. He knew it was the beginning of the end of the life he had known and loved, and it was a giant step into the unknown. Crossing the county line would see this working class family thrust into an alien, middle-class lifestyle. As they entered Hertfordshire, Rose's eyes could not have been wider or brighter as she drooled over leafy suburbs of almost forest-like proportions, and houses with large, green gardens. This most definitely had *middle class* written all over it!

Her mother Harriet, on the other hand, was happy where she was. She had only known life in the East End. She wasn't sure whether a move for her family was the best thing but she wasn't going to stand in the way of her daughter's dream. However, after saying goodbye to her beloved grandchildren, this wise lady took a moment to remind Rose that, no matter how posh she became, she would never take the East End out of her family.

It was obvious that Harriet and Rose didn't really have a close mother–daughter relationship – in fact, when they were together they seemed like magnetic poles, always pushing each other away. The reason for this emotionally charged barrier was Rose's inheritance of her mother's extremely strong character and temperament. That said, the way the two women used their strength could not have contrasted more. The whole of Harriet's long life was dedicated to ensuring righteousness and correcting inequalities whenever or wherever she came across them, while Rose discovered at a very early age that she could use it to get her own way.

Harriet was very fair, as straight as a die and as honest as the day is long. This was exemplified on a rainy winter's day when she was spring-cleaning her house. As she was on her hands and knees cleaning the floor under the dining table, something in the corner of her eye caught her attention. Her table had a scratch. It wasn't a large scratch, but this was the table she reserved for best and only used for special occasions. It was a table she had bought ten years previously, one that she had worked for and saved for over a long period of time. How had she not noticed it before? She knew she hadn't made it, and the position of the damage meant it wasn't made by her family or invited guests, so how did it get there? Then the realisation hit her: the table had been scratched when she bought it! She had paid full price for a damaged table!

Harriet had never been a woman of means and worked hard for everything she owned, so she certainly wasn't going to put up with someone selling her a table that was not of the quality she had paid for.

She went back to the shop, which was still there and still under the same ownership. Fortunately it was the place where she had purchased most of the household furniture, so they recognised her as soon as she went through the door. After being greeted by the shop assistant, she politely explained the situation, firstly to him and then to the owner. They both listened intently, although she could see that the owner wasn't as interested in her explanation as he should have been. She could read faces well, and he was obviously waiting for the opportunity to interject with their standard reply of, 'I'm afraid, Mrs Graham, that after all this time there really is nothing we can do about it.' It was a response that had never failed him before but he obviously had no idea what was coming.

Harriet had entered the shop with only one intention, to get the damaged table replaced, and she wasn't leaving the shop without a faultless new one. It didn't take long and there was no blood spilt before they came to a painless, amicable agreement. The new, undamaged table was delivered the following week and the damaged one collected. Harriet certainly wasn't a woman to mess with but, most importantly, a wrong had certainly been righted.

Within a year of the family moving, however, her life took a cruel twist when her rock and the love of her life, her husband Alfred, died. This was a life-shattering moment for Harriet because her relationship with her husband had been perfect and their life together, although hard, had also been perfect. Their relationship may well have been the reason she did not have such a good one with her daughter; perhaps she had given so much to Alfred that she had less love to give to Rose.

It was quite clear that the day they buried Alfred was the worst one of her life, epitomised by her full-length dive into his grave. Just as the soil began to reverberate against the top of the coffin she could take no more and flung herself down. The resulting physical pain was nothing compared to the emotional torment she was going through.

There were more than enough people to pull her out and brush her down; her small family and her close friends had been joined by over a hundred members of their extended East End family. For the next few weeks Harriet's empty shell remained locked inside her now-empty house. The door only opened to reassure friends and neighbours that all was well, though obviously it wasn't. But ultimately she was a realist and she knew that, although she would mourn in her own way for the rest of her life, she needed to pull herself together. After all, she had three rapidly growing grandchildren to protect from the demon that was middle class!

Much to the excitement of the three boys, and the irritation of a surprised Rose, Harriet packed all her belongings and made the move to foreign parts: Broxbourne in Hertfordshire. Yes, the very same Broxbourne in Hertfordshire that her daughter and family had moved to just over a year before.

To be fair, Harriet was nothing if not considerate, and she moved into a rented house at least eight hundred yards away. Irritating as her presence might have been initially, she became a very useful resource to Rose and offered the help and assistance her daughter needed. The hours Harriet was so willing to provide child-sitting gave Rose time to finely tune her ever improving middle-classness. Mind you, it worked both ways because for Harriet, being with her grandchildren was by far her favourite time and the hours they spent together had a profound effect on a developing Geoffrey. He, in particular, loved her endearing sense of fun and he listened intently to her tales of East End life. That ensured that, unlike his mother, his feet stayed firmly rooted to the ground and they built an unbreakable bond.

The moulding of a middle class family was moving on apace because Cyril had quickly secured a job building and repairing aeroplanes at Hawker Siddeley. The position was steady, and above all respectable, and it was also well paid. It gave him the opportunity when he wasn't working to indulge in the last knockings of his former life through occasional trips back to the East End. With the start of the war not far away, this new job arrived at the perfect time for Cyril. When the call-up eventually came, he had already worked himself into a position that made him indispensable to the company so he was given special dispensation because his expertise was far too important to the war effort at home.

The family benefited greatly from this stroke of luck because, unlike millions of other families, the three boys had their dad at home – a home that would have been under threat from attack night after night if they had remained in the East End. The leafy, suburban Hertfordshire countryside was not high on the Nazi list of prime bombing targets.

Cyril became accustomed to this happy family situation and started to embrace it wholeheartedly far more quickly than Rose could ever have hoped or expected. As his East End ways waned, they were replaced by his often suppressed comedic ability – especially where his boys were concerned.

Not all the comedy was scripted or intended because it turned out that Cyril could turn everyday tasks into slapstick comedy. The Ham family experienced a fine example of this during an air raid. A government information leaflet had recently been pushed through their letterbox detailing the procedure households should implement against a potential enemy gas attack if they had to stay at home when the siren went off. Today the leaflet would appear rather basic, but during the war this was cutting-edge stuff. The incredibly well-thought-out advice stated, with accompanying diagrams, exactly what you should do in the unlikely event that you and your family couldn't get to an air-raid shelter when the siren sounded. In a nutshell, you were advised to hang a wet blanket on the inside of the exterior doors before huddling beneath something sturdy. This could be a place such as the cupboard under the stairs or, less sensibly, under the kitchen table.

The dropping of bombs was a very rare event in rural Hertfordshire but late one Saturday afternoon, just a few days after the leaflet arrived on the doormat, the air-raid siren went off. Cyril took control; after all he had prepared for this moment, he was the one who had hammered a nail in the top two corners of the front and back door frames. Rose had done her bit by placing a thick folded blanket next to each of the doors, with a full bucket of water by the side.

Cyril calmly gathered his wife and three children and ushered them under their sturdy kitchen table and hung blankets over the front and back doors before picking up the bucket by the back door and hurling its contents over the blanket.

This was a moment of great hilarity for his young sons, but it was the look he was getting from Rose that Cyril noticed first. For someone so house-proud, a self-inflicted flood in the kitchen was not something funny. Fortunately for Cyril, there was no scratch on the underside of her table to compound the situation.

Cyril couldn't understand why she didn't applaud his efforts. He'd read the leaflet; he knew what to do. He'd implemented the instructions exactly as he'd read them. The problem was that Cyril was a not a fan of 'The Establishment'; having spent his life getting by using his own wits, a government leaflet was not his idea of a good read. He had therefore 'scan-read' it (his definition). The problem was that Rose had read the whole leaflet more than once, including the bit where it said to soak the blanket in a bucket of water prior to hanging it up.

Fortunately for the male side of the Ham family, this type of comedic behaviour turned out to be hereditary.

Still, war or no war, life had to go on and the time had come for Geoffrey to start his primary education. For him, school years were fun, right through his primary and secondary education. The only real complication occurred when he was fourteen and his mother decided that the family name needed to change. The final pieces of the middle-class puzzle were about to fall into place; the family surname was extended to Hamilton and Rose changed her forename to the much posher Rosa. Rosa and her family were now proper Hertfordshire middle class.

From the very beginning it was clear that Geoffrey was bright, so he didn't really need to apply himself too much to get through his primary education and into Hertford Grammar School. However, not long into his schooldays the Cyril-educated sense of humour came to the fore and he discovered the joy of practical jokes, aided and abetted by his twin brother, Anthony, who followed the same educational path. They quickly learned that being identical twins was a blessing from the Comic on High, and a gift they could use to their best advantage.

Geoffrey's lifelong desire to find humour in every situation started in a fairly modest way at primary school. In cahoots with Anthony, they began with swapping seats in lessons before escalating to collecting double portions of lunch, and then moved on to substituting the more talented of the two into any sporting event they were made to perform. Inspired by these fairly basic successes, which seemed far more risqué to a schoolboy than they actually were, Geoffrey pushed the boundaries even further. He really could see humour in most things and was definitely the ringleader. Anthony was a willing participant and part-time prank co-creator, although he was also often the butt of his older brother's flourishing sense of fun. For Geoffrey, seeing what he could get away with continued right through grammar school and into his years of national service, each prank becoming more daring than the last one.

By the time they were both called up for national service in the RAF, they had shortened their names to the more mature-sounding Geoff and Tony. This was not the only thing that had matured for Geoff; his comedic side, so carefully nurtured by his father and honed at school, had also moved up to the next level. A group of young men, all unsure of what their years of national service had in store, proved to be the perfect platform for him to make his father proud.

Geoff and Tony were sent to Germany for almost the entire two years of national service. Somehow both of them returned with no command of the German language. Remarkably, though, Geoff had achieved a mastery in the use of nail scissors that was not usually associated with young men. Obviously this level of personal hygiene in a proper middle-class boy was something his mother would have been very proud of but, unfortunately for Rosa, Geoff's unique skill with the nail scissors wasn't perfected by expertly cutting finger or toe nails.

He had actually perfected his nail-scissor technique during the many hours it took him to cut the lawn in front of the station commander's office window on his hands and knees. This was the punishment his sergeant doled out for the first heinous crime Geoff committed during national service. He experienced many others throughout his two years, but this was the most laborious. In all the years that followed, he happily recounted this story but always fell short of confessing the actual crime.

Even though he was abroad and doing his duty, the years in Germany were a happy, carefree time for Geoff, something he enjoyed for the entire time he was there – lawn clipping excluded, of course. However, as his time neared its end, he started to look forward to the next phase in his life: higher education and a move into the world of horticulture.

Before heading off to Europe Geoff had applied to Writtle Agricultural College, just outside Chelmsford in Essex, for a place on their national diploma in horticulture. The compulsory interviews had been carried out and his letter of acceptance arrived just before he left for national service. On his return to Blighty he spent only a brief time at home before repacking his bags and setting off for Essex. Tony accompanied him, having also been accepted by the same college but on their agriculture course.

During Geoff's few weeks at home he managed to take and pass his driving test. One of the joys of being posted to Germany was that no driving licence was required to get behind the wheel of a car, so he returned as a relatively experienced driver. All he had to do was to take his UK driving test and he would be mobile. His father had promised to buy him a car when he passed.

The fact that Geoff was young and that he had been hurtling around the German countryside in cars and military vehicles rendered him slightly overconfident when the day of the driving test arrived. He progressed without fault through most of it, perfectly reversing around a corner, turning in a perfect three-point turn and carrying out his hill start as if it were on the flat fens of Norfolk. Finally, his examiner had just one last test of his driving ability to perform.

'Right, Mr Hamilton,' he said. 'The last thing we need to attempt is an emergency stop.'

This held no fear for Geoff; he had been forced to stop sharply on many a German road without skidding or losing control of whichever vehicle he'd been driving.

The next instruction came. 'When I tap my clipboard on the dashboard, I'd like you to stop as quickly and safely as you can.'

Geoff was ready. 'Yes, certainly,' came the rather confident reply from a very polite young man. His mother would have been so proud!

He was primed and ready, so off they tootled down the road. Out of the corner of his eye, Geoff noticed the examiner's clipboard rise and start its rapid descent. With the confidence of an experienced driver, he slammed his foot on the brake and stopped more rapidly – and probably more safely – than he had ever done before. Not a chance of a skid. He was so delighted.

Looking over to the passenger seat, expecting to get the official nod of approval from the man who knew a good emergency stop when he saw one, Geoff couldn't believe his eyes. The examiner was no longer sitting where he had been just ten seconds before. Then he noticed a rather crumpled figure in the well of the passenger seat. It was the instructor, still clutching his clipboard and looking up at Geoff with a rather shocked expression. A combination of not being quite ready for Geoff's early braking and no seat belts in cars in those days, meant he couldn't halt his sudden, forward momentum.

With terror in his eyes and through gritted teeth, the examiner announced that they wouldn't be trying that manoeuvre again. He pulled himself back onto his seat, brushed himself down and they continued back to the test centre in silence.

A short while later, Geoff's driving licence arrived, and with it his independence.

The car Cyril bought his middle son was what was to be expected: a vehicle that would get both Geoff and Tony to college for the beginning of each term and back home at the end of each term. There would be a risk in driving it any further than that!

Even though Cyril backed the decision of their twin sons to attend Writtle, he was concerned that they might not be choosing the right path in life. This concern was well-founded as no member of their respective families had been involved in horticulture or agriculture. Rosa's father had been on the stage before giving it up to become a London cabbie; Harriet's family had been predominantly tobacconists, while on Cyril's side shoemakers held prominence over every other trade. The boys' choices represented quite a shift in occupation. Rosa also had her reservations.

However, just as he had done at school, Geoff passed comfortably through college and gained the highest honour possible at that time, a National Diploma in Horticulture. He was now armed with the knowledge and practical experience he needed to launch himself into the world.

Unfortunately a land-based career was not part of Rosa's middle-class plans. She'd have preferred her sons to become accountants, bank managers or solicitors. Then, in an unforeseen twist, Geoff added to her woes. Spending the evening in London with a group of friends from college, Geoff met a lovely young lady and was smitten. She was a young French lady. *Mon Dieu* – what was he going to tell his mother? To add insult to injury, her father was not an accountant, a solicitor or a bank manager but a soldier in the French army.

Colette's parents had sent her from Paris to London for a year's training in the millinery trade. They thought it important for her future that she learned a trade as well as learning English. What they didn't plan for was their daughter never returning to live in France.

Geoff stayed on at Writtle after completing his course. He had been offered a job in their horticultural department, which gave him the perfect opportunity to hone all the skills he had learned on his college course. He worked there for a couple of years until eventually he decided that it was time to break free and go it alone.

A life as a self-employed landscape gardener beckoned. As if this life-changing decision were not enough, soon afterwards he and Colette were married at St Pancras Registry Office in 1958. Because of Colette's Catholic upbringing, though much to Geoff's dismay, a church service in Paris followed soon after they had tied the knot in London. This was never going to be an easy trip for Geoff as his French could only be described as – well, not very good.

Ultimately, the draw of the family was too much for Geoff and he and Colette settled just a few miles from Rosa, Cyril and Harriet. They rented the Old Vicarage in Ware, Hertfordshire, and soon afterwards son number one was conceived and born. Stephen emerged without any great problems at the beginning of 1961. The next generation had arrived.

Chapter Two

It was Monday 30th April 1962. After eight solid days of landscaping, Geoff felt he needed an evening out to break the cycle of all work and no play. When he arrived home, he had a quick scour through the local newspaper and found the perfect tonic. All he needed now was to persuade Colette to go with him to see a film – *The Guns of Navarone.*

There was a bit of madness in his method because son number two should have arrived by then but was proving a lot more reluctant to emerge than his older brother. Geoff had an inkling that the noise of a war film might help things along a bit, although he omitted to mention to Colette that it was also a film he quite fancied seeing.

Someone really should have told him to be careful what he wished for. Colette had already tried all the popular methods for getting things going – running up and down the stairs, hot baths, a stern talking to her bump, even jumping up and down. A loud film was something she hadn't tried, but she was prepared to believe Dr Hamilton's recommendation.

Son number two had quite obviously decided to make his mark as early as he could on Geoff's life. Not only was he late, but he also decided that halfway through the film the time was right to begin his unstoppable journey out into the big wide world. To be fair, when you're immersed in fluid it's very difficult to hear whether the film has finished or not, so this doesn't help with the accuracy of your timings. Geoff was left with no option but begrudgingly to leave the film early and rush Colette back home.

The 1960s was the era when the phenomenon of home births really took hold and, after the smooth delivery of Stephen by home birth, a plan had been put into place to go down the same route. While Colette continued her waddle to the car, Geoff stopped in the foyer of the cinema to phone the midwife. The chat was brief – far too brief for the subsequent terrifying conclusion. All the midwife needed was an update on the condition of the mum-to-be before she made a potentially life-threatening decision. Life-threatening for Geoff, not his unborn child.

Colette wasn't going to make it home, it was too far. The midwife wouldn't get to her in time, it was too far. The only possible option – and there was no other option – was the closer one: Geoff's parents' house. This struck terror into his heart. His mother was obsessively house-proud and no part of him could visualise a good outcome to this situation. However, he had no choice but to go with it. The next phone call was to his parents, and fortunately it was his father who answered and tentatively took the news. Cyril assured his son that they would be ready by the time Geoff and Colette arrived.

With considerable reluctance and filled with pure, unadulterated terror, Geoff set off in the direction of 34 New Road, Broxbourne after squeezing Colette into their Austin Morris 1300. The fear of his mother's reaction to the inevitable mess seemed to calm any worries Geoff had about the impending birth. As he drove, his head was filled with images of how pristine his mother's carpets were, the pure, crisp white sheets on the bed, the sparkling bathroom (including bidet) – the list was endless!

Fortunately the midwife had arrived first, so Rosa was on her best and most helpful behaviour. The spare bed had been readied for the main event. The sheets and quality blankets had been removed and towels laid in their place. After a fairly short period of time a head appeared – my head – and was quickly followed by the rest of me. It was not the most exciting entrance, but an entrance all the same.

Mind you, if Dad thought life with me was going to be that easy he should have known better. I was already late, but this was soon forgotten when I refused to breathe, which was odd really considering the quality of the middle-class Hertfordshire air. This lack of desire to get my lungs working went on far longer than Dad, Mum or the midwife expected, but that's the trouble with middle-class air: you're never quite sure if you're allowed to inhale it or not.

I started to turn blue and, after a couple of moderate taps on the bottom from the midwife, I turned even bluer. She thrust me towards Dad and after three good, hearty smacks on the bottom we bonded, at precisely the same time as my lungs sprang into action.

Whether it was allowed or not, the middle-class air was sucked into my lungs. Apparently I cried for a couple of minutes and then nodded off, which gave a little insight into the rest of my life. It turns out that nodding off is a natural gift I was born with, a talent that can be displayed unintentionally at any given moment but very often at the most appropriate time. Dad was very envious of my ability to drop off when we visited Rosa and Cyril and quizzed me often to try and understand how I did it.

From a very early age Dad called me by the nickname he had given me. I don't actually remember exactly when this started, just that I have no recollection of him ever calling me anything else. Being a young and innocent lad, I always thought it was reference to my rather firm and pert bottom but Dad knew differently. He took great pleasure in knowing what it meant and, most importantly, knowing that I didn't. It was only when I reached an age where I could understand that he explained that it was nothing to do with the pertness of my bottom and everything to do with my legal name.

Dad wasn't particularly religious so, as the christening service began, his mind drifted away from the event and to wondering how I would grow up. He tuned in just as the priest attempted to drown me in the font and heard him speak my name – Nicholas. Suddenly, there it was; there was the humour and he recognised what a fantastic result it was. Dad's uncontrollable Hamilton brain had spotted that his middle son's name could be broken down into two parts, Nickel and Arse (Nickel-arse).

He was now in overdrive, every brain cell focused on finding a way to use this amusing combination, and he quickly found it. 'Tinbum' was the nickname I was given there and then by my own father.

It was typical of Dad to find humour in a serious situation, particularly where humour should have played no part. Growing up, I didn't understand this hereditary affliction and I still don't really understand it now. I can only trace it back to Cyril because the rest of that side of the Ham family had passed away before I was born. I do know, however, that I've been saddled with the same curse.

Having to find something humorous in any situation, then feeling obliged to share it, should be listed as a medical condition. If it's genetic, surely it can't be helped. Therefore it's not my fault. That said, not everyone agrees with this explanation. Some people feel these genes of mine are, quite frankly, the wrong genes – but I'm absolutely certain that they are most definitely the right genes!

Chapter Three

In 1964 we were on the move. Dad had decided it was time the family invested in bricks and mortar of its own. Mum was horrified. She wasn't particularly interested in investing in a house; to be honest, she didn't seem particularly interested in investments at all, though she did play the football pools every week, if that counts. The other problem she had with this grand plan was that it had Rosa written all over it.

The only thing that needed to concern Mum about this potential investment was that the family couldn't afford it. Dad also knew they couldn't afford it, but owning your own home was a sign that you were doing well and he liked that idea even if it wasn't completely true. There was definitely a large part of Rosa in that attitude!

In order to finance the move, Dad borrowed money from our neighbours without Mum's knowledge. Roger Smith was the manager of the farm next door and he, his wife Jan and their two children had become good friends, good enough for Dad to feel he could ask to borrow money from them. However, he was a man of great moral principle and if he was going to borrow money he was going to do it properly. He couldn't afford to appoint a solicitor to draft a legally binding contract so he drafted his own, stating how much he'd borrowed, how much he was repaying, the amount of each instalment and the date of the last payment. He signed it and exchanged it for the rather large sum of £400. The same amount his parents had also spent on their first house.

Even with the benefit of this generous loan, our new home was not on the grand scale of Rosa and Cyril's semi-detached house in Broxbourne. Dad knew that he could never afford Broxbourne, let alone a house that was only supported on one side. We moved beyond the cheaper end of the town to the village of Wormley, 14 Wharf Road to be precise, where we settled in a two-bedroomed terraced house – supported at both ends! We were still a bit posh, though, because to the rear of the property we not only had a garden with a path, but we also had a shed.

Rosa could have happily highlighted these rather smart embellishments of our working-class property to her growing clique of middle-class friends in an attempt to elevate it but she didn't because, in order to access them, you had to walk past the outside toilet. Apparently an outside toilet was not something middle-class ladies of the 1960s aspired to.

These facts, plus a few hundred more, were the reasons why this branch of the Hamilton clan were never going to aspire to the heights Rosa had set and remained firmly and happily working class.

Dad was still a landscape gardener, while Mum had her hands full at home with three young sons, so money was tight. Things seemed to progress without much change, apart from the inevitable bursts of growth and energy from us boys, although Mum was helped through these by Great-grandma Ali. This was the only name we knew for our great-grandmother Harriet and it had evolved long before, when she was young. Although christened Harriet as a child, this was soon shortened to Arri, eventually became Ali and was adopted by all who knew her.

She was now in her mid seventies, but every day she walked the mile from her house to ours to see if Mum needed any help. She was happiest looking after us boys but was also willing to do the shopping or cleaning. It wasn't long before her sleeves were rolled up and she would get stuck into two important jobs: the chores and wearing us out. Once both had been satisfactorily completed, she would walk the mile back home. With the addition of baby Christopher to look after and Dad at work all day, Mum's unpaid home help was very much appreciated.

On the face of it, with finances tighter than a ballet dancer's pouch, having three young children was probably not the best thing to do at this point in their lives. However, Dad was proving to be both resourceful and innovative. There is no question, in my mind, that these early experiences of no money, many mouths to feed and small bodies to clothe were the catalyst for his later televised speciality of always being able to come up with cheaper ways to create whatever was required, albeit in the garden. The old gardening adage of 'making the best of what you have' was something he adopted as his philosophy for life.

Although all of his children were affected, unfortunately the person this frugal lifestyle affected most was always going to be his youngest child. A combination of rapidly growing children and the cost of clothes meant that Christopher was the main victim of the (mostly home-made) hand-me-downs. Mum was an avid knitter and sewer so we never had to go out naked, even if we couldn't afford to buy new clothes. In fact, I still have my knitted winter balaclava (we all got one), which was not only indispensable to keep those cold winter winds from freezing your delicate ears but was also an essential fashion item for a young 1960s' lad – or so Dad kept telling us. I loved mine, not because Dad told me that it elevated me into fashion's elite few but because it made me look like Lancelot and definitely the better looking of the three Knights of the Round Table in our house.

It would be another twenty years before Dad became known for his continuous stream of budget ideas. By then he'd moved from 'things for the family' to 'things for the garden', showing millions of amateur gardeners that rather than buying, they could make them instead. His contraptions were simple. He could turn his hand to almost anything, a skill he definitely honed on his children.

The first somewhat substantial Geoff Hamilton budget creation was the bunk bed. Plans were drawn up and a small scale model made to ensure it worked. Why go to such lengths? Well, this was no ordinary bunk bed; this was top-notch – and it could be separated into two single beds when required. Dad always had an eye on the future, so he went the extra mile with this construction. He was confident that his name as a quality landscaper would spread, his income would rocket, resulting in the inevitable move to a more palatial residence. Rather than all sharing one room, we three boys would have a room – and therefore a single bed – each.

This was the reason he always gave for making the bunk bed in that way, though I'm not so sure. Over the next thirty years, all too often I witnessed (though I never really understood) his obsession with wooden dowels.

Those of you who remember the things he made during seventeen years of *Gardeners' World* may have noticed that, almost without fail, each one incorporated a wooden dowel. The bunk bed was no exception: the bottom of the legs of the top bed and the tops of the legs of the bottom set were drilled and a dowel slotted into the tops of the bottom bed. The top bunk could then be positioned with no fear of movement. This magnificent construction not only outlasted our time in Hertfordshire but also saw Stephen and me through our teenage years as single beds, before being given away – no doubt to be made back into a bunk bed to serve another set of children. If nothing else, Dad made things that lasted!

While he was constructing it, I don't think he imagined the years of conflict this bunk bed would provide between his two older children. It was Stephen's first vehicle for trying to assert his older-brother status. Being the oldest, he was given the choice of top or bottom bunk as his night-time domain. Unsurprisingly he chose the top bunk, thus confirming his status in the hierarchy. It was just assumed that I'd be all right sleeping in the bottom bunk. Fortunately, as soon as I saw this Herculean construction, I'd already decided the bottom bunk was for me. I've always felt safe close to the ground.

It wasn't long before Stephen realised that by using a newly discovered and perfected acrobatic technique he could hang down from the top bunk and talk to me. Now, from the day I was born I've always needed a good night's sleep so this wasn't something I welcomed or encouraged.

Stephen was aware of my need for sleep, so it wasn't really surprising that he took the opportunity to irritate me by trying to keep me awake. However, Dad had trained me properly in coping with irritating people. He had schooled me well in his tried-and-tested method, honed over many years of torment from his own older brother. His method was quite simple: it was to do nothing. He told me that this reaction would irritate the irritator far more than they could irritate me.

This piece of advice was meant to help at school but instead I put it to the test with Stephen. The passive approach worked a treat and it was great to turn the tables on my older brother, especially as I didn't have to put in any effort. I'm not renowned for doing nothing and not putting in the effort, but in this case it worked like a dream.

I'm told that I've always had a very strong will from the day I was born and turned blue. Some might call it stubbornness, even obstinacy, but when I set my mind on something I invariably see it through. Stephen had not taken this into account. I could lie in bed, pretending to be asleep, for as long as it took for him to become really irritated and give up.

On the memorable final occasion of Stephen's top-bunk dangling, he must have been so irritated that he lost mental control and loosened the grip of his legs under the covers. Suddenly he hurtled past me head first. There was a loud thud and a muffled yelp. Clutching his head, he leapt up and scrambled back onto the top bunk.

He knew that he should have been asleep and any commotion would alert Dad downstairs, resulting in him venturing up the stairs to see what had happened. The muffled yelp didn't work; as Dad moved slowly up the stairs, we could hear every footstep and every creak of the stairs. I desperately tried to quell my giggles at having witnessed the floor coming up to meet Stephen's downward plummet. I knew the trouble he was going to be in – and me too, if I was discovered to be still awake.

By the time Dad made it up the stairs, I was pretending I'd been asleep for at least an hour but Stephen was still flushed from his sky dive. It didn't take long for Dad to prise out of him what had happened and it left him with only one option. During their subsequent trip to A & E, the doctor stated that no damage had been done – although in hindsight, I'm sure it's the reason for him turning out the way he has. Needless to say, he never top-bunk dangled again.

A short time later it became apparent that ridiculing those who have suffered an unfortunate incident, such as a headlong dive to the floor, can come back and bite you on the posterior. It was during the following summer, when the three of us were enjoying a brotherly but competitive game of cricket on the narrow strip of lawn we called our back garden. This was not as easy as it may sound, primarily because Dad had erected a second-hand climbing frame that took up almost half the grassy space. It had been given to him by a very satisfied client whose children were now too old to use it.

Dad was well aware that there were opportunities for freebies, if you happened to be in the right place at the right time, and this climbing frame was definitely one of the best. He was also aware that sometimes you need to put your hand in your pocket. This was one of those moments. No matter how tight finances were, some things in life were essential for your children to get the correct social education.

His pockets were long so he had to dig deep, but he bought us a proper cricket set. He told us it was the best money could buy because it was from Woolworths. At that age he could have told us anything and we'd have believed him – and he often did! The set comprised three stumps (no bails), for one end, one stump for the other, a bat and a tennis ball. Dad called it 'top-notch' and told us we'd be the envy of every child in Wormley.

Things were going well until Christopher, on his turn to bat, was out first ball to a beautiful delivery by yours truly. If I'd have known the definition of a 'perfect googly' at such a young age, that's how I'd have described it. It most definitely was a pearl of a delivery. Before coming into bat, Christopher had been fielding for some time in the outfield (the concrete path that ran down the side of the grass) and he wasn't keen to go back there. He dared to protest the legitimacy of this perfect delivery. We had no umpire and he wasn't listening to his older siblings who, at six and seven years old, were far more learned in the laws of the game.

I wasn't going to continue arguing; it was my turn to bat next and that was that. I decided that, as he wasn't budging from the crease, my only option was a sit-down protest. I was prepared to sit on the edge of the lawn until he was prepared to see reason and hand over the bat. What I hadn't anticipated in my plan of passive action was that the little devil would opt for his own method of protest – violence! From behind me, with as much force as he could muster, he brought the bat crashing down on top of my head with an almighty thud. It was a life-defining moment; during the few seconds that followed I realised what a very hard head I have. No pain!

The aftermath of this shocking crime revealed the bottom half of the cricket bat lying on the garden path. Christopher was standing there agog, with the handle of a bat still in his hand. There was absolute silence, shattered by me shouting, 'NOW LOOK WHAT YOU'VE DONE!'

Christopher dashed into the house crying and Dad appeared to see what had happened. This time there was no trip to A & E and not even a visit to the doctor; he just rubbed my head and told me I'd be fine. He knew that it would take an awful lot more than that to damage my head.

The bat, however, was a different matter. It was not something he could fix and certainly not something he was prepared to replace, having only recently spent money on a 'top-notch set'. We had to make do with a bat cut out of a single piece of wood that was lying around, the handle roughly rounded by rubbing it with sandpaper. Obviously this is the reason my England cricket career was nipped in the bud; my younger brother has a lot to answer for!

Chapter Four

Looking back at those early years, what affected me most profoundly was Dad's determination that we should understand the value of everything and appreciate all that we had. Our see-saw in the back garden was a fine example of this. It was nothing special, just a rusty frame that Dad had found somewhere, and the wooden seats had long gone, but it was a see-saw and that was all that mattered.

We were made well aware that this was the only see-saw we would ever have and we had to look after it. I didn't have any friends with see-saws in their back gardens, which made it even more special. My brothers and I spent most of our time outside, so the see-saw and climbing frame were the focus of our activities, particularly now that cricket was out of the question.

If Dad had paid for either of them, he'd certainly have had his money's worth. The savings he made on these items left him with enough spare cash to invest in a cat, two guinea pigs and food. It won't come as any surprise that our two dark-brown guinea pigs were housed in a 'Geoff Hamilton special'. He made the hutch and run out of odd bits of wood and eventually placed it in the corner of the garden, out of reach of children propelling themselves off the climbing frame.

The cat was jet black and Dad named her Pushkin. We didn't know why but readily accepted the name. In hindsight, calling a female cat after a male Russian poet doesn't make a lot of sense, unless you're a big fan of Russian poetry.

She was female, not spayed and not likely to be because of the cost. She was a lovely cat, energetic, tolerant of children, intelligent and good-looking – all the elements any parent would hope for in their own children. But, as with children, these are the ones who cause problems.

Pushkin was so good-looking and so intelligent that it was only a matter of time before she attracted the attention of an equally good-looking tomcat. Something Dad should have foreseen happening. Saving money by not having her spayed proved a false economy and she fell pregnant. Worst of all she was pregnant with no means of support because the father had disappeared.

For the next two months we had a less energetic, less slimline and less tolerant cat until six bundles of fun appeared. It was just what Dad needed – a large litter. Being young children we were captivated. The guinea pigs were forgotten; the see-saw sat on the path unused and getting rustier, while ivy started to cover the climbing frame. The kittens were far superior to any toys we had.

Things just got better when they were allowed to go outside. Even at that young age, they were intelligent enough to know what time of day we returned from school because each day they were waiting for us in the garden. Every day after school we had no time for our friends, preferring to race back home to our beloved kittens.

We were having so much fun that fortunately none of us thought about naming them. I say fortunately because Dad had known from the time Pushkin fell pregnant that he'd have to give away all her kittens because we could only afford one cat. This sort of feline trafficking was not something we'd experienced; we believed we were keeping all six. Then disaster struck.

On that fateful day we returned home from school at our usual time, having run all the way. We ran straight into the garden to play with the kittens – but there were only five of them. As they charged around the garden we counted them several times, independently and simultaneously, but there were definitely only five.

Panic set in and we found Dad, who also made it only five. He concluded that the missing kitten must be hiding somewhere in the garden or was maybe in the house. We looked in the shed, the guinea pig run and hutch, all over the house, Mrs Clarke's garden next door and even in the outside toilet, but our sixth kitten was nowhere to be seen.

Dad was starting to struggle with the rising emotions of his three boys, when suddenly a small black kitten appeared on the horizon, slowly heading towards our back gate. The three of us rushed out to greet our late arrival, thankful that he or she wasn't lost and lonely somewhere in the Hertfordshire countryside.

As we got closer it was obvious that something was wrong. Stephen noticed its tail – well, half of it. He couldn't see the other half because it was hanging down behind the remaining stump. We rushed back to get Dad who, in his typical no-nonsense fashion, collected the kitten, told us it would be fine and whisked it off to the local vet in a cardboard box from the shed.

As he drove the injured kitten there he bemoaned the fact that, unbeknown to us, it was only a matter of days before the kittens would be collected by their new owners. An unexpected vet's bill was something he wasn't looking forward to receiving.

He soon returned home with a groggy kitten that was still nodding off in its cardboard box. We all peered in, Mum included, and were shocked to see that what had been the start of an elegant black tail was now a short black stump. More than half the tail had gone.

To break the shocked silence, Dad announced that he (confirmed by the vet) would now be known as Bobtail. Dad knew what he was doing; this momentous declaration left us more than satisfied and the trauma of that afternoon soon became a distant memory.

When the weekend arrived, Stephen and I hatched a plan to hunt down the suspected villain of the piece, a Siamese cat that Dad had identified as the vicious attacker of our defenceless little Bobtail. We didn't have the necessary commando gear to do this properly, so opted for green shorts and T-shirts. We looked for clues but, after four fruitless hours of fingertip searching, we concluded that the cat must have got wind that Wormley's top commando team was on the case and fled in terror. We had no idea what we'd do with it if we found it, but it seemed the right thing to do in defence of our beloved Bobtail.

Gradually, and very craftily so that we didn't notice, one by one the kittens disappeared. Dad took the opportunity to use Bobtail as a smokescreen for his kitten trafficking; soon five of the kittens had gone. We were convinced that Bobtail would stay forever; after all, who'd want a cat with a stump for a tail? Well, it turned out that the blooming tail-removing vet did!

The day Bobtail was collected was the saddest of my very short life, but we were convinced that he was going to a good home and would be loved as much as we loved him. It was a good fifteen years later that Dad sheepishly confessed that during the tail removal, he had agreed a cat swap with the vet. He would wait for the earliest opportunity to convince his children of the benefits of rehoming Bobtail, after which the kitten would be returned to the vet – and the vet would waive the bill.

For a week I was bereft, then a tortoise arrived. Granted, it was not the most exciting or unusual of pets, but it was completely different to anything we'd had before. Most importantly for those who held the purse strings, it was cheap to feed, though they hadn't considered that it had a life expectancy of eighty to ninety years. The tortoise was only in his thirties, so the responsibility for its care in its dotage was laid fair and square on the shoulders of the children. I'm not sure why I stepped forward to nurture and protect this new pet throughout its life – maybe I was still traumatised by the loss of Bobtail – but Dad very quickly closed the deal.

We never knew what sex it was, although based on the amount of lettuce it consumed it was probably male. In the end my commitment to lifelong care was cut short because the ungrateful tortoise decided to go off and find a better home. He was certainly determined, having already made half a dozen escape attempts only to be retrieved a few yards down the road. To this day I wonder whether it was my poor attempts at creating a palatial hibernation home or the very basic menu of lettuce that spurred his bids for freedom. Maybe he'd just decided that the lettuce was greener on the other side of the Hamiltons' fence.

Chapter Five

To escape this menagerie of pets and children, Dad popped out to the local rowing club once a week for a night out with his rowing friends. He was a keen rower, something he'd discovered while at Writtle College, so becoming a member of the Broxbourne Rowing Club was a given and he always tried to row at weekends. On the face of it, these weekly nocturnal excursions seemed harmless enough but they were not as innocent as they seemed. It was in the rowing club bar that Dad had his first brush with the law.

It was a fairly routine Thursday evening and the five friends were relaxing in the club lounge (*sans* family, pressures and worries) when the local bobby appeared. Being a member, Clive was not an unusual sight in the rowing club but he never attended in full police uniform. As he slowly and somewhat embarrassingly approached Dad's group, they knew the sight of him in full rozzer regalia didn't bode well.

After the initial pleasantries were dealt with, Clive's demeanour changed as he got down to police business. With a rigid finger he pointed sternly at Martin and said, 'It's you I've come to see.'

This came as a shock to Martin, who considered himself a pillar of the community. The rest of the group, Dad included, breathed a sigh of relief even though none of them could remember a recent minor misdemeanour that would have resulted in this official visit.

After reading out the details from his notebook, Clive revealed that he had come to arrest Martin for non-payment of a parking fine. That was news to Martin. After consulting his notebook again and double-checking the dates, Clive gave the exact location and date of the offence, as well as the date when the resulting fine should have been paid. Then, to add insult to injury, he also gave the dates of two letters that had been sent to remind Martin to pay this outstanding fine.

Martin was his friend so Clive pointed out in a somewhat melancholy tone that unless he could stump up the money there and then, he would have to arrest him and taken into custody. He would be incarcerated until someone could pay the fine for him or he appeared in front of the magistrates.

Horrified, Martin frantically searched through his wallet, the pockets of his trousers and his jacket, even though he knew he'd spent his last bit of cash on the pint of beer on the table in front of him. Looking at his uniformed friend and rowing companion, he asked whether he could pay the fine in full the next day when he received his weekly pay packet, but apparently the law waits for no man.

As if telling off a child for running in the school corridor, Clive told him that he'd had more than enough opportunity to clear his debt, and the station sergeant had given strict instructions that he must come back with either the money or Martin in handcuffs.

In the 1960s the Hertfordshire police obviously took a dim view of poor parkers and, even more so, poor payers. In an attempt to help his friend (in an official capacity, of course) Clive mentioned that the money just had to be raised; it didn't all have to come from Martin himself. That was music to Martin's ears, and he saw the prospect of a night in the police cells disappearing as quickly as the beer in his pint glass. He turned to his friends – surely they would bail him out with the £2 he needed.

They also looked in every pocket, but the most they could muster was only £1.

Then Dad had a great idea. They were regulars at the club and he was confident that he could persuade the barman to make up the difference with a short-term loan from the till. Apparently there were rules, however, that meant he couldn't.

Martin realised that this left PC Clive with no option but to get the cuffs out and take him away. Head bowed and arms held out in front of him, he waited for the click of the manacles. His friends watched as PC Clive did indeed put his hand in his pocket – but instead of pulling out the cuffs, he pulled out a crisp £1 note. He thrust the note into Martin's hand, with a warning that if it wasn't paid back by six o'clock the following evening, he could look forward to a long spell in the police cells.

This Samaritan-like gesture meant that Clive could release himself from an awkward situation. The money was duly paid back the following day, well before the deadline.

That a police officer who had come to arrest someone for non-payment of a fine ending up paying most it himself fitted Dad's sense of humour perfectly. It could have been written by the Monty Python team, his favourite type of comedy, and it was a story he told over and over again to anyone who cared to listen. Mind you, this was a minor brush with authority compared to the several speeding fines Dad amassed over the next twenty years.

Dad had just bought a Ford Granada Estate, a car with far more power in first gear than his little Austin Morris had at full throttle. This was somewhat worrying to me, although he never understood why, because during the whole of my young life his driving style was one that required his accelerator pedal to be pushed firmly to the floor. That had been the only way of getting any speed in the Austin, but these newfangled machines were different. In the Granada, the pedal-to-the-floor technique released a G-force – that car went like a rocket!

It was a beautiful summer's morning and Dad was making the most of it. He'd been pottering in the garden when he suddenly remembered he had a meeting in Melton Mowbray in twenty minutes, half the time it would take to get there. Still in his work clothes, he leapt into the Granada and sped off, leaving his home at Barnsdale in a cloud of dust behind him.

He shot off down the lane. The main Melton Mowbray road was clear when he turned onto it with his foot pushing the accelerator pedal to the floor. To get to Melton Mowbray, he had to pass through Oakham, the county town of Rutland. Because he was late, he took no notice of the 30mph speed-limit signs. He zipped through Oakham, down the high street and out the other end.

Suddenly, over the noise of the pumping pistons of his massive Granada engine, he heard sirens behind him. His reaction was like everyone else's in the same situation: his foot pinged straight off the accelerator and he looked for somewhere to pull over to let the emergency vehicle get through. As he pulled over into a farm gateway, he expected blue flashing lights and sirens to fly past him. When that didn't happen, he looked in his rear-view mirror and saw that the police car had pulled in behind him.

As Dad continued to watch through his mirror, what can only be described as a man mountain eased himself out of the driver's door of the police car. With muscles rippling beneath his uniform, he approached the Granada. Not wanting to delay his journey, Dad didn't get out of the car to meet the advancing police officer but stayed put and wound down his window.

With a beaming smile, the officer casually strolled to the car – and at that precise moment Dad knew he was in big trouble. It really isn't a good sign when the officer in question opens with, 'Good morning Stirling Moss, do you know what speed you were doing?'

'Yes, officer, thirty miles per hour,' was Dad's hasty reply.

The officer laughed for what seemed like an eternity. Once he'd regained his composure, he left Dad in no doubt that he'd been driving at an average speed of just under sixty miles per hour, right through Oakham town centre.

Oakham was then, as it is now, only a small market town and therefore not particularly busy on that Thursday morning but Dad realised that couldn't be used as a reason for his speeding. Instead he started to tap his speedometer, muttering, 'Bloody thing can't be working properly.'

The policeman burst into fits of laughter yet again. He was obviously a very jolly policeman but he wasn't giving an inch as he announced that he had no option but to book Dad for speeding.

Even when faced with the laughing policeman and no sign of winning, Dad wasn't one to give in easily. He countered with, 'Would it help if I said that the British police are the best in the world?'

'No,' came the very quick and now not so jolly reply.

Not put off, Dad continued, 'But honestly, if this was

America you'd have hauled me out of the car and I would be lying prostrate on the bonnet of my car with a gun pointed at my head. In any country in South America, I might not have had the chance to speak – they're more than likely to shoot first and ask questions later. What if I was in an Arabian country? My driving days could be over because and for a little bit of speeding I could have both my hands cut off as a penalty. And what if…?'

'Oh, just f**k off,' came the reply as the policeman turned back towards his car.

Even though Dad was in full flow and somewhat unwilling to terminate his off-the-cuff support of the British constabulary – he still had a lot of countries to get through – he took the opportunity to wind up his window and gently pull away. Out of sight, he put his foot down, in case the policeman changed his mind! He was so pleased with himself and he dined out on that story many a time.

The retelling of this great escape had a big effect on Dad's twin brother, Tony, so much so that, unfortunately, he never forgot it. Some years later, having been stopped by the police for speeding, he remembered his brother's successful monologue almost word for word and decided to try his luck. Just as the policeman told him the speed he was doing and that he was going to issue him with a ticket he burst into the same patter.

'Would it help if I said the British police were the best in the world?' he started.

He got no further. The officer butted in, 'Are you

trying to bribe me, sir?'

It wasn't the outcome that Tony was expecting. Panicking, all he could think of to say was, 'No, officer, just book me.'

Unlike his brother, Dad seemed to have the ability to be in the right place at the right time, obviously with the right policeman and definitely with the gift of the gab.

The problem he had controlling cars had actually started ten years earlier, when I was six, Stephen was seven and Christopher was four. For some strange reason, each time we got into the car we always sat in age order, even though it wasn't something we had been told to do. This seating arrangement unnerved both my brothers because that left me in the middle and I had a problem with the smell of petrol fumes. They made me feel nauseous, which generally resulted in me being sick in the car. Although my brothers were wary of this, I was a very thoughtful boy and always made sure my head went between my legs if I ever felt the initial swell of the tsunami in my stomach.

As the Austin Morris was the only vehicle we had, it was primarily Dad's work vehicle. Whenever we got in, we were surrounded by the tools of his trade. Generally the larger ones, such as the spade, fork, rake, etc., were taken out for family trips, but the small hand tools were in the well running behind the front seats. Now I'm older and wiser, logic tells me you that if you have a son who suffers from car sickness this wasn't a good place for them to be. To make matters worse, on arriving back home having erupted en route I was always made to clean up. Some years later, when talking to the owner of these tools, I was told that cleaning them was an attempt to correct the car sickness. It didn't work!

Stephen was the keenest on this seating format because it meant that, sitting next to the pavement-side door, he was always first out when we arrived at our destination. Christopher either had to wait until his roadside door was opened or he shuffled across once I was out. As it was 1968, there were no seatbelts in the car so Stephen was often out before Dad had pulled on the handbrake.

One particular Sunday, we were making the short journey to Broxbourne for lunch with our grandparents. As usual, I jumped into the car first followed by Stephen while Christopher was walked round to his door by Dad and the door closed behind him. Once Mum had locked the house and we were all settled, Dad fired up the Austin and we were off.

Just as the car started to move forward, Christopher shouted, 'Dad, Dad, my door isn't quite shuuuuuuuuu—' and he was gone.

Realising what had happened, Dad did an emergency stop and leapt out. Taking half a dozen steps back to where Christopher was laying in the road, he bent down and asked, 'Why did you do that?'

Shocked from the fall and confused by the question, Christopher got up, dusted himself down and climbed back into the car. This time Dad slammed the door shut to make doubly sure it wouldn't swing open again and off we went. Dad didn't get into a flap and wasn't an overly emotional person but, as described earlier, in a farmer's gateway just outside Oakham, he knew exactly the right thing to say – ridiculous or not.

Chapter Six

It was Monday 4th September 1967, and I was dressed in my uniform ready for my first day at Wormley Primary School. From the moment my tiny bottom hit my tiny seat, I took to school like a duck to water – although more like an eider duck having to cope with an occasional stormy sea.

Being easy to get on with and a sociable boy, I had lots of schoolfriends, but my best mate was Nigel Bateman. We clicked from day one, although at the time I didn't know that his father Ralph was a rowing friend of Dad's. During the first two years of school Nigel and I were inseparable: we sat together in class; we were on the same team for football in the playground and always played together. This was a partnership not to be broken – or, at least, not until that fateful day.

The teacher we'd had for two years decided it was time to move on to another school, and a brand new teacher arrived to continue the good work he had started. His name was Mr Maguire. He was bit older than the previous incumbent – he must have been at least thirty – so to me he was ancient.

He came with fixed ideas, determined to do things his way, and his first job was to rearrange the class. He was in charge, a superior figure to us children, if nothing else because to us six-year-olds he was at least ten feet tall. The first round of relocations came and went without much trouble and without disturbing Nigel's and my cosy partnership. We continued to sit like two peas in a firmly closed pod. Thinking we were safe, I looked to the front and to my horror noticed that Mr Maguire's right arm was outstretched and his long, slender index finger was pointing directly at me. It was a mightily long finger and the catalyst in an unjustified divorce.

'Nicholas, can you move to sit next to Angela, please?' were the words that came out of his mouth, words I really didn't want to hear.

'No, I don't want to,' came my rapid and forceful reply.

Mr Maguire repeated himself. 'Nicholas, can you move to sit next to Angela, please?'

My reply was the same as before. Rather than turn to Nigel and move him, our teacher wanted to assert his rightful authority, so he tried once more but got the same determined response.

This insubordination was more than he could bear. Now very red-faced, he moved up to the next level. 'If you don't move, I'll have to move you myself.'

I was staying put but, before I had the chance to tell him that, his long legs started to move towards me and there he was, standing behind me, grasping me firmly by each arm. He lifted me upwards but I'd beaten him to it and grabbed the sides of my seat. Up I came, chair and all. Mr Maguire started to shake me to try and detach me, but the more he shook the more firmly I gripped. I gripped as if my life depended on it, which it probably did.

Obviously our teacher was a madman; that was the only explanation for his attempt to move me away from my best friend and next to Angela. Not that there was anything wrong with Angela; she just wasn't Nigel.

Rather than take me, chair and all, to my new Angela-based location, Mr Maguire decided to escalate the situation to the very top level. 'Nicholas, if you don't let go of the chair and move next to Angela, I'll have to take you to see the headmaster. I know he will take a very dim view of this.'

Unperturbed, and resolute in my fight for the rights of the little people, I didn't loosen my grip and stayed glued to my chair. That was it; off we went to see the headmaster, chair and all.

I was plonked unceremoniously in front of the head-master and Mr Maguire explained the situation to him in great detail. I sat still and quiet. At one point, I'm sure I noticed a slight twitch of the headmaster's mouth that could have passed for a smile. It made me feel he was on my side. However, after being fully briefed, the headmaster informed me calmly that if Mr Maguire wanted me to move it was for a very good reason and I must do as I was told.

I was asked if I understood and I nodded, although my hands were still firmly gripping my chair. I was returned to the classroom by Mr Maguire, still attached, and placed back in my original space next to Nigel. Why Mr Maguire didn't do the sensible thing and put me next to Angela while he had the chance, I'll never know.

I have no excuse for what happened next; it was very much out of character and wasn't planned. There was no thought process involved and in the blink of an eye it just happened.

Once Mr Maguire had returned to the front of the classroom, he started speaking in the triumphant tone of a man who knew that he'd won the battle. He was determined to show the rest of the class that he was in charge and asked me again to move. The problem was that it had been a long walk to and from the headmaster's office, and on the way back there had been time for all reasonableness to be replaced by stubbornness.

I sat still.

That was definitely the straw that broke the teacher's back. Like a cheetah at full speed, he moved from the front of the classroom. Gripping both my arms, this time he lifted me out of my seat, stood me up and frog-marched me towards the classroom door.

Our school was brand-spanking new, built on one level, and it ran the full length of a large playing field. The playground was in the middle of this field, and our classroom was just beyond the bottom right-hand corner. The door Mr Maguire marched me to opened directly onto the path that led to the playground.

Once out of the classroom, and the door firmly shut behind us, Mr Maguire wagged his finger at me and told me what a naughty boy I was for not doing as I was told. I'm not sure at what point during his tirade I found myself throwing a punch, but throw a punch I did.

I can't offer an explanation for this reaction because I wasn't a violent boy. It was almost like the cheetah had cornered his lunch, an unwitting warthog (my legs have always been too short for me to liken myself to a gazelle). He had pushed me to the edge – to a point where I feared for my life. He was standing facing me and, as I was only six and short-legged, the area of the impact isn't hard to imagine.

Just like any animal faced by their most feared predator with lunch stamped on their forehead, I instinctively began to run. I heard a yelp followed by a groan from behind me, but I didn't look back.

My little legs were going like the clappers. I ran diagonally across the playground, heading for the path that took me to the outer gate and then out of school. As I cleared the playground, freedom started to come into view. Feeling almost safe, I took this opportunity to look back. I suppose I expected to see Mr Maguire disappearing into the distance back to the classroom, but there he was steaming towards me.

My head went down, my concentration focused on speed and I forged onwards. As I flew through the gate onto the pavement, I took a last look back to see Mr Maguire was standing at the gate, steam coming out of his ears, but not able to leave the school grounds. He must have almost been within touching distance when I reached the gate, but I was now free!

When I stopped running, I wasn't sure what to do next. In my short life I'd never found myself in this sort of situation before; all I knew was that I couldn't go back to school. Once the panting had subsided, and after careful consideration, I realised that the only option was to go home. I knew that, after my detailed explanation, Mum would understand.

When I got home, the back door was unlocked but Mum was nowhere to be seen. Deciding nobody was home, I ventured into the lounge where I found Dad sitting in his chair. This was an unexpected turn of events since he should have been at work. Peering over his newspaper at someone he wasn't expecting to see at home at that time of the day, he asked why I wasn't still at school.

What happened next was his own fault. He was always lecturing me to tell the truth so I did, confident that he would understand. I was sure he would write a letter to Mr Maguire that very morning, telling him that my place was next to Nigel.

As a young child, inexperienced in the workings of the human body, seeing the blood drain from someone's face in such a rapid manner was strange and surprising. Dad was still in his seat but the newspaper had dropped onto his lap and his face now resembled the colour of a white bed sheet. It seemed to take him forever to respond, and when he did, he spoke very quietly and with a slight quiver to his voice. He asked me to confirm what I'd just said, so I did and he went even whiter.

After a couple of minutes of silence, he asked me to get in the car. Off we went. I had no idea where we were going, but I was sure things would be all right once Dad had returned to his normal colour.

We travelled a couple of miles to a service station. Once out of the car, we went into the eating area and sat down. Normal facial colouring had now been resumed. It was a typical 1960s place with red faux-leather seats that were very cold on the bits of my legs not protected by my grey school shorts.

I could see Dad was deep in thought, so I didn't disturb him with the question I was dying to ask: why were we here? We only ever stopped at service stations to get petrol, usually when travelling to and from our camping holidays, but this time was different and we'd gone inside. Why?

After a few minutes a waitress appeared, and not long after that so did a Knickerbocker Glory. I was gobsmacked – a Knickerbocker Glory!

This was Dad's masterstroke, and something that perhaps the United Nations should take note of, as it seems that negotiations progress much better over a Knickerbocker Glory. It wasn't a reward but a negotiating tool and I was like putty in his hands. As I scooped all the ice cream from the tall, fluted glass with the longest spoon I'd ever seen, Dad began.

He explained in a rational and clear manner why I should do what I was told at school, including moving seat if my teacher asked me to. Most importantly of all, I should never punch a teacher – or anyone else, come to that. He was clear that no matter how wrong they might be, punching was never the answer.

With my mouth full of Knickerbocker Glory, all I could do was nod. Of course I knew he was right and I couldn't argue with such a beautifully constructed piece of wisdom. He was right, I was wrong and, yes, I would go back to school and be a good boy. I was under the influence of that massive glass of ice cream. Mind you, the 'violence is never the answer' bit of wisdom should really have been said before I punched my teacher!

We both got up, my bare legs peeling from the faux-leather seat as if it were a giant plaster, and tootled off back to the car before heading in the direction of school. Once parked, we walked hand in hand towards the headmaster's office; I'm assuming Dad held my hand so that I didn't do a runner.

Dad explained that whatever problem there was had been sorted out and that I would do as I was instructed, for which the headmaster was very grateful. The first hurdle had been negotiated successfully but we were about to face the second and more difficult hurdle.

Tentatively we set off towards my classroom. Dad knocked then popped his head around the classroom door. Once he had Mr Maguire's attention, he indicated that he needed to talk to him, so the teacher asked the class to continue reading while he went out of the room. Casting a glance in Dad's direction and then mine, his hands moved to protect his nether regions. His brow furrowed and his expression became sterner.

Dad launched into his apology for any pain I had caused, both mental and physical. He explained that I had promised that from now on I would be the perfect pupil. For me it was a bit galling really, because apart from this minor blip, I was a perfect pupil.

I watched as Dad set off across the playground and up the path, the route I had taken just two hours previously. As he disappeared into the distance, I went back into the classroom with Mr Maguire a pace behind me all the way. I made my way to my seat next to Nigel, expecting to be told to move – but nothing was said or done.

The good news is that I sat next to Nigel for the whole of my time at the school, while continuing to be the perfect pupil (blip excepted) and I believe that Mr and Mrs Maguire went on to have several children, so no permanent physical damage was inflicted.

Much as I hate to admit it, the reason for this whole violent episode can be laid fairly and squarely at the door of Great-grandma Ali. There can be no doubt that the stubborn streak I inherited came from her line of the family, and so did my ability to throw a punch. Being an East End girl, boxing was weekly entertainment in

Ali's family and something she remained keen on all her life.

As well as being Mum's free home help, she turned out to be useful in other ways. Whenever Mum and Dad needed a night out, it was always Great-grandma Ali they turned to as a babysitter. She had no qualms about being in her seventies and having the responsibility for looking after three young children. Being the youngest, poor Christopher was put to bed before they went out, so he missed out on Ali's evening life-training sessions.

She was left with strict instructions that the remaining two children could stay up for another hour, but had to be in bed by 8.30pm. Dad had experienced her babysitting skills when he was a child and he was well aware that her timing could be flexible. We only had a radio in the house, as was the case when Dad was a child, so we children were her evening's entertainment.

Great-grandma used to wait until my parents had got into the car before reminding us that we could stay up until they returned, provided that as soon as we heard the car pull up outside we dashed upstairs, jumped into bed and fell asleep straight away. We agreed wholeheartedly to this plan, but it had a critical flaw. As usual, that flaw was my older brother. For a reason only known to him, Stephen couldn't get into bed without the light being on. Every time we dashed into our bedroom, he flicked on the light before clambering up to the top bunk.

Prior to the mad dash up the stairs, Stephen and I spent the evenings playing games with Ali and telling her anything of note that had happened at school so she was up to speed with our lives.

Being a woman well-experienced in life, she felt we had reached the age where we needed to learn self-defence. That Christmas, we had each received a pair of boxing gloves as her present from Father Christmas so we generally started the evening with a game then moved quickly onto Ali's favourite form of entertainment, boxing. You would never have known that she wasn't a qualified boxing referee. We boxed according to her two main rules: no punching to the head, and don't punch too hard. Despite being simple rules, my older brother seemed not to understand either of them.

The referee was definitely in charge, so each match went on as long as she allowed. Once the final round was finished, we still had time for a couple of board games before we heard the Austin Morris 1300 pulling up outside the house. That was our signal to depart rapidly.

Even from outside of our terraced house, Dad could hear the sound of a herd of elephants charging up the stairs, and just by standing on the pavement and looking up he didn't have to wait long before our bedroom light came on. The result was always the same.

Dad had known before he left the house that the babysitter would once again disobey his rules and allow her charges to stay up late. He also knew that it was his eldest son who couldn't get into bed without turning on the light. He also knew that he had to pretend to be unhappy that Stephen was still awake. He appeared never to discover that I was pretending to be asleep – the skill I had grasped from an early age and one that Stephen never mastered.

Ali's lifelong love of boxing started when she was a child, and she loved listening to it on the radio. When she was babysitting us, she was particularly keen on the new wonder-boxer from America, Cassius Clay, and she used him as the template for my boxing skills. Consequently I blame Great-grandma Ali and Cassius Clay's fabulous straight right punch in equal part for the devastating blow inflicted on my teacher. If only Mr Maguire had known sooner about my nocturnal activities!

Chapter Seven

Life tends to have a way of putting problems in your path even at such a young and tender age, so it wasn't long after this heroic display of friendship towards Nigel that our bond was tested – by a female.

There was a goddess in our class and her name was Julie. Both Nigel and I liked her a lot, and at seven years old we were both obviously mature enough for a long-term relationship. It all came to a head one day in the playground, when her friend told her that we both wanted to be her boyfriend.

I have to admit that she took some persuading but finally, and much to Nigel's dismay, I got the girl. I'm certain my model-like good looks and my knobbly knees swung it. I started life as quite a good-looking boy, which didn't go unnoticed – I'd already been the face of Whiteley's Food Store. (I think I should mention at this point that my face played no part in the store's eventual closure.)

Dad's older brother, Barry, had his own photography business. When he was offered this commission he needed a male model and he chose me; obviously I was the best-looking of the three brothers! Believe it or not in the 1960s stardom and celebrity, even if it was gained by advertising fruit and vegetables, got the girl.

By playtime the next day Nigel had forgotten about the previous day's tension and normal service was resumed; no female could ever get in the way of our friendship. However, at the end of school each day Julie and I walked hand in hand across the playground and up the path to the outer gate. Not a word was spoken. I wasn't perplexed by this silence; the most important thing was that we were together. We lived at opposing ends of Wormley so, when we reached the outer gate, she went one way and I went the other.

After the relationship had been going strong for at least two weeks, it was time to make my intentions known. When Dad arrived home from work, I announced that I had some great news – I was going to get married!

His reaction was not quite as I'd expected or hoped for. Rather than congratulating me, shaking my hand and telling me what a good choice I'd made, he disappeared rapidly from the room. For what seemed like an age I was left standing alone in the middle of the lounge, still full of joyful anticipation about what married life would bring.

Dad returned slightly redder in the face and with a beaming grin on his face. He could barely talk coherently, but he managed to ask me to get in the car. I had no idea where we were going, though I suspected it was to see Julie's parents to set things in motion. It soon dawned on me, however, that we were travelling the same route as we had just a few weeks earlier.

We drove the same couple of miles to the same service station, and even sat on the same faux-leather seats. I knew what was coming but not why. The Knickerbocker Glory duly arrived, the long-handled spoon sticking out invitingly from the ice cream. I didn't need to be told and was digging in before Dad had started to thank the waitress for her speedy service.

His attention turned to me. Strangely enough, he seemed much more comfortable giving this piece of fatherly advice than the previous one. He started by explaining the responsibilities of getting married, the cost of both the wedding and our subsequent life together, as well as the need for a good education. He finished by suggesting that we put our marriage plans on hold until we were in our twenties, telling me that if she was 'the one' then she'd be happy to wait.

Although he put it very eloquently and simply, I was confused. There was no problem about money because I was in employment, getting ten shillings pocket money a week for the jobs I did around the house. The responsibilities of married life seemed achievable to me. However, after a little more encouragement I conceded to his better judgement. I knew our love was strong and Dad was right: waiting thirteen years wouldn't be a problem.

Two weeks later Julie was Nigel's girlfriend and I seemed destined for bachelorhood. I never did get to tell her of my marriage plans. Dad, however, was relieved to hear about my new-found single status.

Diplomacy was one of Dad's great skills, but there was no question that he could dish out punishment when he had to. We were brought up very well, and from day one all three of us had great respect for our parents. This respect stemmed from honest and reasonable discipline (Dad's definition, not mine) when necessary, and he generally dished out the penalty when it was required. There were definitely times when he seemed to enjoy that part of parenthood a little too much. The result was that we tried our hardest to be good because we didn't want to risk having to face his terrible punishment.

This disciplinarian side to Dad's character reared its ugly head one lovely summer's evening not long after he had returned from a hard day's landscaping. He was weary and needed a cup of tea and a few of his favourite biscuits to restore him. Unfortunately, on this particular day this scenario did not play out as he'd have liked.

My brothers and I had arrived back from school also tired and in need of a nutritional pick-me-up, but our dinner wasn't ready. We sat on the settee hoping that there was a biscuit or two left in the tin that we could share. The appearance of this tin was rare, and generally only happened when guests visited, but today Mum was standing in the doorway holding onto what definitely looked like the sacred biscuit tin.

After she handed it to me, Mum disappeared. I removed the lid in the hope of finding at least three biscuits in there – always the easier option because Stephen never quite mastered the art of breaking a biscuit into two equal halves. (And yes, he did always manage to keep the bigger half for himself.)

Once I'd opened the tin, the shock of its contents stunned all three of us into silence. It was like discovering the Holy Grail: it was full of BOURBON BISCUITS! If I'd not been pinned between my two brothers on the settee, I would have jumped for joy.

Dad had a real weakness for Bourbon biscuits, which is why we had them in the house even though they were far too posh for our little house. The only time we were able to nibble on a Bourbon was when we'd been particularly good and we were handed one each as a reward. If Dad wasn't at home Mum occasionally raised that to two Bourbons each, but that was as rare as the mighty Spurs coming top of the First Division.

I'm sorry to have to do this, but I have to point out that the blame for what followed rests firmly at Mum's door. Rather than handing a single Bourbon to each of us, she emptied a full packet into the tin. What was I supposed to do? Temptation had been laid firmly into my lap.

I declared that this should be a two-Bourbon day. With the tin so full, I knew that Dad would never notice a few missing biscuits. Unfortunately, we adopted the following method of counting and distributing these heavenly biscuits: I put my hand into the tin, removed six biscuits and distributed two to each brother and left two for myself. Stephen did the same and so did Christopher. We had indeed only each removed two Bourbons from the tin for our own consumption; the only problem was that this method totalled eighteen biscuits.

In our defence, Mum left us with all that temptation for a full ten minutes before returning. I handed back the biscuit tin. She was surprised by how light it felt, so she lifted the lid and looked inside. Just two lonely biscuits were left in the bottom and she was not amused.

I can't speak for the other two, but I knew what I'd done and I knew there would be consequences. All she needed to say was, 'Just wait until your Dad gets home.' That was enough to have me trembling. We were left on the settee for only half an hour after that, but it seemed like a week as we waited for the executioner to appear. It was excruciating sitting like three convicts on death row.

I heard the back door open and the kettle being filled with water and switched on. The tea cup hit the worktop hard, while the cupboard door creaked as Dad reached in for the teabag. The sound of the lid being removed from the biscuit tin was unmistakable.

Dad looked in and found only two Bourbons. That was odd; he thought he'd finished them off the day before. Opening the cupboard again and reaching for a new packet, he was surprised to find that it had disappeared.

This was it: it was the time for the testimony that

would send us down for the crime we had committed. Mum filled him in with the gory details. She was only cross because we would be too full of biscuits to eat the dinner she had lovingly prepared.

As she spoke, Dad looked forlornly at an almost empty biscuit tin. Fully briefed, he slowly got to his feet and appeared in the lounge doorway. His right arm rose gradually, until it was horizontal. His index finger slowly unfurled until it was rigid and pointing towards the stairs, at which point he uttered one word: 'Bed.'

Suitably sentenced, heads bowed, we marched off to bed. The punishment had been delivered. It wasn't an 'up to your room to play' type of punishment, this was a proper 'get into bed and stay there' punishment. Dad knew how effective it would be and, at the end of the day, the punishment fitted the crime. These were BOURBON biscuits after all.

I was fairly full of biscuits, but missing out on an evening meal was still devastating because most nights they really were something to behold. There were two great assets to your Mum being French: the summer holidays in France were great and, more importantly, her cookery skills were something else. Even on a tight budget she could whisk up fabulous meals day after day.

Food was important to me, so when one mealtime finished I immediately started looking forward to the next one – until I was served up something I didn't like or couldn't eat. From as far back as I can remember, if ever I mentioned I wasn't able to eat something on my plate, Dad's official line was quite clear: 'Your mum's a very good cook and there is absolutely nothing wrong with the food she serves, so you'll sit there until you eat it.' Somewhat uncompromising and some might say harsh. However, as I got older I realised what a great line it was. I was never undernourished, and I'll try any type of food and eat virtually everything. Obviously there are foods that I would choose above others, but I've turned out to be a very unfussy eater and I put that down totally to that one line of Dad's.

There was, however, a big flaw in his stance over Mum's cooking: because it was so uncompromising, he never understood that my body couldn't take rhubarb. I couldn't get anywhere near it – just the smell of it cooking made me retch. Fortunately, even though everyone else in the family loved rhubarb, it wasn't a pudding Mum served often. On the rare occasions we did have THE FOOD OF THE DEVIL served as a pudding, I would remain seated at the table with those words still ringing in my ears, knowing that I would be there for some time.

I knew the procedure. I always poured custard over the rhubarb to dull the smell, then I pushed the bowl as far across the table as I could get away with. These simple actions helped to dull the acrid odour. Then I waited for everyone else to finish, lick their bowls clean and leave the table, whilst I remained in my seat to wait. I waited, and waited and waited; I waited until the clock ticked round to eight o'clock, bedtime. At that point, I was allowed to remove my bowl from the table, take it to the kitchen and go straight upstairs to bed. To this day, I still can't get anywhere near the evil stuff.

There was a worse punishment, reserved for the worst possible crimes. Dad didn't have a sadistic personality, but he took great pleasure in doling it out to his children. It came in two parts, with the selection of which one being dependent on how dastardly the offence had been. The first, and lesser punishment, was the Quick Death. This was reserved for crimes committed against the state. By far the worst punishment was the Slow Lingering Death, which was reserved for crimes against Dad. As the creator and distributor of these punishments, he knew he had the power to act in a godlike way. Occasionally he found it in his heart to give us the choice as to which punishment we wanted, even though death was always the ultimate result.

The executioner positioned the offender in the same position, irrespective of the punishment to be administered. You would lie full length on the lounge floor, generally in the middle of the room, always well away from any breakable objects. The Quick Death involved a one-minute burst of rapid tickling, with the tickling fingers generally concentrated around the midriff. However, the Slow Lingering Death was far more calculated and was a minimum of three minutes of much slower tickling, always finding every ticklish part of your body. The net result – crimes against Dad became quite a regular occurrence.

Crimes against Mum, although under the same juris-diction, sometimes resulted in the severity of punishment they deserved, but sometimes not. There were no set rules. It all seemed to depend on a combination of the initial crime and how funny His Excellency Judge Dad thought it was.

A perfect example of this happened between my two brothers, a situation where I was completely innocent. I say 'completely innocent' because I wasn't even at home, although I played a crucial part in the crime. I was attending a friend's birthday party, which was due to finish at 6pm. The friend's house was only five minutes from ours, so Mum dashed along to collect me. She had asked Mrs Clarke next door to keep an ear out for my brothers while she was out. Mum had left Stephen and Christopher at the dining table eating the meal she had prepared for them. They each had a lovely plump piece of fish, covered in a thick white sauce with mashed potato, carrots and peas.

I was ready for collection when she arrived, so she was only out of the house for about ten minutes. In that time, war had broken out. On our return, we were greeted with Stephen pinning Christopher into a corner of the dining room and a piece of fish, still covered in its thick white sauce, slowly sliding down the wall behind the dining table. It was clear to see where the point of impact had been; it was at the other end of the long, glutinous slime of white sauce.

Apparently it had taken Stephen only minutes to

irritate Christopher to a point where all he could think of was to threaten to cause him damage with a piece of fish. Not just any piece of fish, but a piece of fish covered in white armour-plate and propelled at breakneck speed by his fork.

However, Christopher hadn't taken into account that Stephen had started studying physics at school. He was aware that any viscous liquid would reduce the natural aerodynamic capabilities of the said piece of fish, giving him plenty of time to duck out of the way. The fish flew, Stephen ducked and the wall took the whole impact. It played out exactly as Stephen had hoped.

On our return, Stephen immediately pointed out the fish. Christopher, now released from his older brother's hold, protested his innocence and blamed Stephen for making him do it. Mum wasn't impressed and sent him straight to the bedroom, saying Dad would be up to talk to him later.

It wasn't long before Dad came home. When told of the recent kerfuffle, he said nothing; he just turned and left the room. On his return, his face wasn't quite as red as when I had told him of my upcoming nuptials, but it was definitely redder than when he had left.

Unperturbed, Mum asked him to go upstairs and talk to Christopher about his behaviour. Even though Dad was impressed by his youngest son's original retort that aggravated his brother, he did as he was asked and explained why propelling sauce-covered fish at his brother was not such a good idea.

Dad knew that any leniency would only cause greater problems, so he then went and had a word with Stephen. He too was sent to bed. It seemed to be a fair outcome to a rather (un)savoury event.

In the 1960s, a 'clip round the ear' was seen as a means of quickly indicating to children that whatever they were doing was not acceptable. It wasn't a smack, it was more of a prod. As a child, Dad had received this punishment a few times from Cyril and it was something he continued with his own children. Although rare, it did happen. Unfortunately he wasn't very good at it and always seemed to clip the wrong child's ear. When told of his mistake by his aggrieved and innocent son, his answer was always the same, 'Well, that's just in case you *do* do something.' At the time, that seemed a perfectly reasonable thing to say.

It took a few years to realise that the old devil always had an answer for everything. Well, almost everything. I've managed to render him speechless several times over the years with some gobsmackingly off-the-wall things that I've done. A fine example was when I decided to recreate a story from the Bible and crucified my Action Man on Good Friday. I made a perfectly fitting crown of thorns and, using red Airfix paint, applied blood at the relevant points. He was then attached to the crucifix I'd made from a couple of bits of wood I'd rescued from Dad's shed. I hung the whole thing on the outside toilet door.

Having popped to the toilet, on his return all Dad

had to say to me was, 'Why?' After more than fifty years, I still don't have an answer for that one.

There were, however, no questions asked when I showed my inquisitive streak. I was a child that always needed to know 'what would happen if…' This particular hair-curling event stays very vivid in my memory. It remains my crowning glory of stupidity, with my only straw of comfort being that I was just four years old at the time.

To me, it seemed such an obvious question to ask, 'What would happen if … I stuck this knife into the electric socket in the dining room?'

I discovered the answer very swiftly. After carefully inserting the knife into one of the holes of the plug socket, unexpectedly there was a loud bang and a puff of smoke. I found myself on my back a couple of feet away, staring up at the ceiling.

Mum rushed into the dining room from the kitchen to see what had caused such a loud noise. Concerned, she bent down to see if I'd been hurt while Dad appeared from the lounge. He stood quietly and surveyed the scene. He could see me lying quite close to the wall socket, knife still in hand and black stuff on and around the socket, so it didn't take him long to work it out. He said nothing, preferring just to give me that 'what have I unleashed on the world?' look, before returning to the lounge.

At the time I wasn't intelligent enough to understand the lasting effects my knife skills would have on my future. Quite obviously, if I'd been intelligent enough then I wouldn't have done it…

Prior to this incident, if my hair needed cutting I was whisked round the corner to our local barber. Once I was sitting on the short plank of wood that was perched across both arms of the seat and adorned with something that resembled a poncho, I was shorn like sheep. It was always a number-three clipping all over.

This changed when we moved from Wormley to Kettering in 1971. We had moved to a modern estate house and were the second family to live there. Around the corner from our house was a row of shops, like all good estates had then; a newsagents, a Spar and three other shops that seemed to change hands on a regular basis. The one thing this row of shops didn't have was a barber's.

Mum was no hairdresser but she decided, with no prior training or instruction in the art, to take up my hair-cutting duties. We had no clippers in the house so she used scissors – not professional hairdressing scissors but the kitchen scissors. The main difference, now that my hair was being cut using scissors rather than electric clippers, was that it was allowed to grow longer. It was at this point that I realised I was the only one in the family with quite curly hair. Could this be a long-term effect of my 'knife in a socket' experiment?

If it was, it was fortunate I stopped after just one attempt; another experiment might have led to me spending the rest of my life with poodle hair!

Chapter 8

Even before I could crawl I was perceived to be a healthy active child, not sickly at all – apart from in the car, of course. Therefore, when I came down with a sore throat and cough, Mum took me to see our local GP, Doctor Bilby.

Surprisingly, despite a trip to see Dr Bilby generally involving being stabbed with one vaccine or another, this was always something to look forward to because he had the biggest jar of Smarties that I'd ever seen on his desk. He really did know how to bribe young children.

He gave me the usual routine check, including the stethoscope he'd just retrieved from the fridge, while I was chomping on half-a-dozen Smarties. This routine check became less routine when he stumbled across a murmur from my heart. My quick check then became a much more thorough going-over – although with no added Smarties.

The result was an appointment being made for me to see a heart specialist at Hertford General Hospital for further tests to determine the source of this murmur. After an electrocardiograph and further examination, they decided I had a hole in my heart.

There were no obvious signs of the defect. Visibly I was no different to any other child and did everything a perfectly healthy child would, except for the annual visits to Hertford General Hospital for a check-up. There was never any question in Dad's mind of treating me differently to my brothers and he never really spoke about my heart problem. I wasn't given anything to compensate me for this life-changing news – no comic, no toy, no special trip to the zoo and certainly no Knickerbocker Glory!

It wasn't long before the inconsistency in Dad's distribution of gifts reared its ugly head. At the age of five, Christopher was admitted to hospital with tonsillitis and, in those days, they whipped out your tonsils as soon as this happened. He was kept in for observation so ended up with an overnighter on the children's ward.

We visited him on his first evening, once the offending tonsils had been removed. This was a family visit to lift his spirits, but I came away very jealous of my younger brother. I know I should have been a more caring and considerate seven-year-old, but I couldn't help it. I wasn't jealous of him being admitted to hospital; that was old hat to me, as I'd been three times in the previous two years. It wasn't because he'd had his tonsils out and was now the centre of attention, as I've never been an attention-seeker myself. It was the gift of a Britten's plastic giraffe that sent me into a fit of jealousy. These were prized possessions and each of us was amassing our own collection of animals. They were received as Christmas or birthday presents only, but suddenly tonsillitis seemed a valid means of acquisition. In my mind, this fatherly act was surprisingly profligate.

As I grew up my heart diagnosis altered several times until, when I was fourteen, they concluded that it wasn't a hole in the heart but possibly a narrowing of the aorta or an obstruction. To discover if this was the case, I was sent to see Dr Gribbin at the John Radcliffe Hospital. He concluded that part of the diagnosis should involve an angiogram.

In hindsight, I would probably say that the combination of a teaching hospital and the use of only a local anaesthetic wasn't the best for a fourteen-year-old boy. It didn't start well. In the ward I was given a gown to put on that consisted of two short-sleeved arms and two ties, so that it could be attached behind the neck and easily removed on the operating table.

It was a great design for that purpose, but the designer hadn't factored in the Lewis Hamilton effect. I hopped onto the waiting trolley and the porter took us down to theatre at a speed I wasn't expecting – we were either late or the hospital porter was practising for a supermarket trolley dash. I'd been aware of the precariousness of my gown when I put it on, so I had tucked each bottom corner under each leg, certain that this would fix it down.

We'd only travelled half the length of the first corridor

but we were already into sixth gear. I gripped the sides of the trolley as if my life depended on it, and it probably did. As we hurtled along corridor after corridor, people leapt aside to allow us through.

The orthopaedics department was full of older ladies. With precision timing, my gown decided to come away from its moorings and do an excellent interpretation of a yacht sail. All fear of falling from the trolley disappeared; the priority was now restoring my dignity.

Eventually I managed to take control of my gown, leaving a trail of very surprised ladies behind me. As the gown lowered, I caught a glimpse of a sign that said 'Theatre', with an arrow pointing to the left. The final corner, although safely negotiated, was done so on two wheels!

The porter had got me there, a bit frazzled and aware that there were now many women who could recognise me – though not by my facial features. In order to make it look like he'd done his job professionally, he sedately pushed me through the double doors and parked the trolley adjacent to the padded theatre table.

Once moved from trolley to table, I was disrobed and four pieces of material used to surround my right groin – fortunately, my vitals were well and truly covered. Once the local anaesthetic had been administered in came Dr Gribbin, all togged up and ready to go. He was my heart specialist and I had full confidence that he would look after me.

We had a little chat, presumably the process doctors

go through to calm any nerves the patient might have about the procedure. He disappeared down into my crotch area, scalpel in hand and after having made a couple of little cuts, one into a vein and one into an artery, he briefly rose, looking very satisfied with himself. A quick word to his assistant and suddenly he had in his hand what I can only describe as two lengths of flexible gutter pipe! Even at age fourteen it was a very disturbing scene, peering down the length of my body to see a man rooting around in my groin area as he pushed these tubes up from my groin all the way to my heart.

The plan was that, once in place, they would use the tubes to squirt in dye and then X-ray the heart to highlight any imperfections before checking the healthiness and pressure of the valves.

In all the commotion, I'd forgotten where I was. This was a teaching hospital; a seemingly non-stop procession of trainee doctors started to appear, all decked out in their pristine white lab coats. One by one, they moved towards the area being worked on and had a good long look at my groin area. Each of them seemed to give a quiet but definitely disappointed 'Hmmm'. After so many young people looked at my groin I would have hoped for at least one 'Wow', but none was forthcoming. I tried to ignore it and returned my focus to the job in hand and Dr Gribbin.

Aged nineteen, and after a second angiogram as well as lots of other tests, the results were finally in. The definitive diagnosis was a growth causing an obstruction under the valve in the heart, just below the aorta – a subaortic stenosis. The conclusion: open-heart surgery was required to remove it.

I was duly booked into the National Heart Hospital in London for my operation and everything went according to plan, apart from three things. Although booked in to be operated on the following day, when I arrived on 31st July 1981, there was no room at the inn. Well, more accurately, no room in the adult ward, but thankfully a bed was available in the children's ward. As I was deemed to be just out of childhood, that was me sorted.

I was obviously the granddad of the ward, with nobody else being over seven except the nurses. Once I'd decanted my belongings from my bag, one nurse took me off to a side room to take some blood. I was wearing a short-sleeved shirt due to the British heatwave, so there was no need to roll up my sleeve. She prepared the syringe and as she approached my bulging vein with her needle she looked up and said, 'You really don't need to look if you don't want to, you know.' I was quite happy watching and told her so.

She proceeded. Blood duly taken, she turned to me with the broadest grin I'd seen and then I realised why she worked on the children's ward. She announced, 'I've never had a patient as good as you before so, as long as you promise not to tell anyone else, I'm going to give you two sweets instead of one!' Suddenly, this potentially life-changing experience had got a whole lot better.

The operation took place at seven o'clock the following morning and I was operated on by Mr Donald Ross, the most eminent heart surgeon of his day. As you would expect from the 'top man', the operation went according to plan.

After a spell in intensive care, followed by the recovery ward, I was despatched back to the ward. This time it was the men's ward, where I would recuperate for fourteen days. This was when problem two all too quickly became apparent.

Still tired and dozy from the operation, I was fast asleep when I was placed in my bed. The following morning, after emerging from my comatose state, I was welcomed by a very chatty bloke in the bed to the left of me. For the first day this was great; it was nice to have someone close who was happy to make friends. If nothing else, it passed the time while I drifted in and out of sleep, although I only managed to squeeze in a reply twice.

On my second day I was more compos mentis. Apparently I was now an equal part of the conversation, but it quickly became clear that he must have had a restraining order against him getting within a mile of anything equestrian because not only could he talk the hind legs off a donkey but the front ones, too. I couldn't understand how anyone could talk for so long without stopping to take breath. I used my childhood 'pretending to be asleep' technique from day three until he was discharged.

A long time later, as Mum got older and had been living on her own for some time, I realised that she could do the same. Then it dawned on me how both of them did it: they obviously breathed by osmosis.

The third problem became apparent when my first meal was delivered to my bedside. The National Heart Hospital was very small with an expertise in all things cardiac but obviously no expertise in cookery, as it had no kitchen. All food was provided by an outside catering company and, as is usual in most hospitals, meals were ordered the day before.

I had encountered two meals that weren't great but were just about edible. On the third day I was eagerly awaiting my order of bangers and mash with a side order of beans – there are times in life when you've just got to spoil yourself. My chatty man next door had left mid-afternoon, so I got a chance to watch a bit of athletics on the ward television and contemplate my delicious dinner prior to mealtime.

My culinary delight arrived at 5pm. There they were, two plump and tasty-looking sausages on top of a mountain of mash surrounded by a sea of baked beans. I grinned from ear to ear before tucking in.

My euphoria was short-lived and turned to utter disbelief. The mash had been made from Smash! Now, forgive me if I'm wrong, but I always thought that a hospital should provide food that helps you recuperate and I couldn't see how substituting reconstituted fake potato for real potatoes could do that. I ate the plump sausages and beans but left the pile of reconstituted spud, piled high on the plate.

Fortunately Dad phoned that evening to say that he was coming down to London the following day to see me and did I need him to bring anything? All he got was a four-word reply: 'just bring me food'. I was starving to death! It wasn't unlike Dad to leave it to the last minute to inform me of things that were about to happen, otherwise I'd have written out a shopping list instead of leaving it up to him. He was my dad after all; surely he'd know what to get me? He and Mum had been divorced for five years by then, so he was used to shopping in a supermarket. What could go wrong?

Dad arrived just after lunch the following day, which was a relief, as I'd spent the last hour picking at a very unappetising plate of food. Like a knight in shining armour, he appeared through the ward doors, life-saving carrier bag in hand. It was so full that I could see the food bursting out of the top. I couldn't wait to get my hands on it and finally consume some decent, healthy grub.

He stood rigidly in the doorway and refused to move until I put my pyjama top back on. It was August and hotter than ever, so all the windows were open and I was airing the massive scar I had on my chest. It was this that Dad couldn't bear to confront – he was so squeamish.

As soon as I was suitably attired, he was happy to move forward. I filled him in on the non-gory details that had happened since my operation. He spent the time removing each item individually from the bag, insisting on interrupting me by stating what each one was. I couldn't really complain, because each item was a lifesaver and something that I liked – although not necessarily what I would have purchased for someone recuperating in hospital.

There was Camembert, sliced salami, rollmop herrings, a wedge of Stilton cheese (loosely wrapped), sliced garlic sausage, some weird and wacky French cheeses, as well as many other quite pungent edibles. He'd quite obviously stopped at the local delicatessen and not the supermarket on the way to the train station.

As a result of my operation I found it difficult to move my torso, so Dad stowed the food away in my bedside cabinet but not before a pungent cloud filled the ward. It wasn't that I was ungrateful for this delectable parcel of foodstuffs, but when I needed to eat I had to open and close the cabinet door so quickly to minimise the odour release that I often grabbed the wrong thing. It was a difficult manoeuvre to complete in my condition.

I'd been expecting more. I know I was nineteen and twelve years had passed, but I hadn't forgotten the tonsillitis episode. Christopher's minor operation equated to a Britten's plastic giraffe, but for my major, life-threatening operation there was not even a plastic meerkat! I'd waited twelve years for the opportunity and, when it came, Dad missed it.

Fortunately I was young and repaired quickly so they let me out of hospital in only ten days, but in that time I had lost a stone in weight, although that would have been a lot more if it hadn't been for the calorific value of the Dad-supplied outside catering. In the weeks, months and years that followed my return home, friends and family were interested in seeing the magnificent piece of scalpel work adorning my chest. All except Dad. His squeamishness stayed with him. Even when the scar had completely healed, he couldn't bring himself to have a look.

Chapter 9

Dad brought in the pennies we survived on, which meant working at least six days a week, so the burden of doing all the shopping was Mum's. It wasn't just the shopping she had to carry, she also had the additional hindrance of three boys in tow. Even at such a tender age, there were times on those shopping trips when you had a distinct feeling that your parent would be happier with one less son to cope with.

Shopping and three young boys was problem enough, but Mum didn't drive so whenever we went shopping we always travelled by bus. For me, travelling on a red London bus was always a great adventure, even if the end result was being dragged around shops or a supermarket.

On a sunny, autumn Saturday, Mum had planned a trip to the Brent Cross Shopping Centre and, as Dad was working, we also had to go. It meant a long ride on the 32A red bus – what a joy. Shopping done and Mum loaded up with bags, we got back on the 32A for the return journey.

I didn't notice leaving North London and travelling

through the leafier Hertfordshire roads because I was engrossed with the boy opposite, who was playing with his Action Man. More importantly I wasn't aware that the bus had pulled up at our stop, or that Mum, Stephen and Christopher had vacated their seats and were heading off to the exit at the back of the bus. Apparently I was told that we were getting off, but that went in one ear and rapidly shot out of the other. What can I say? I liked Action Man, even though I'd crucified mine.

Suddenly, just as the bus started to pull away, I noticed my family had disappeared. I leapt up from my seat and ran to the back of the bus. There I was, standing on the platform, holding firmly onto the central pole with the bus moving and Mum shouting 'jump'. Jump? Was she mad? The bus was moving.

I hung on to the pole as the bus sped up. Mum dropped her bags, left my two brothers with them and ran as fast as she could after the bus until it reached the next stop. I safely alighted and walked back with a panting mother by my side to the pile of bags and brothers. I couldn't believe that she would use such an obvious method of reducing child numbers as leaving one on the bus. Her only redemption was that, at the vital moment, she obviously realised that she'd left the wrong son on the bus!

It certainly seemed, as a child, all modes of transport were problematic for me and this situation certainly didn't improve when I got my first bike. This was such a wonderful occasion, even though it had been handed down from Stephen and was therefore third-hand by the time I got it. It meant I was mobile and the world was now my oyster. Once Dad had reattached the stabilisers, I was off. This mean machine was sky blue and of a size where my toes, at full stretch and pointing downwards, could just about reach the floor. It didn't have anywhere to attach a hand pump because it didn't need one; the wheels were made from solid rubber.

After a few weeks of racing around, well stabilised, it was decided that I was ready to go it alone. It fell to Dad to run several marathons holding the back of the bike seat while I wobbled up and down the garden path until I wobbled no more.

It was then that the solid tyres proved their worth. I could go anywhere – and certainly places my older brother couldn't – with his flash, pneumatic tyres. I could bounce up and over kerbstones without any damage to my indestructible wheels. I have subsequently realised that Dad passing the bike to me may have been another part of his wider plan; kerbstone bruising of the vitals was inevitable and the annihilation of my reproductive organs a possibility – he was such a cunning man.

Inevitably my legs grew, although only fractionally, and the bike became too small. This left Dad with a problem. If the testicle-thwacking, solid-wheeled bike was to be passed onto Christopher, he needed to provide me with another. As Christmas wasn't far away, it would be the perfect opportunity to kill two birds with one stone: my main Christmas present and a replacement bike in one.

We were no different to most families, as Christmas was always an event in our house, but ours was a short-term one. We didn't put up our tree or decorations more than a week before the day itself and they came down a week afterwards. The most important part of Christmas for Dad was that the presents remained a secret. Knowing what you were getting prior to opening them was never an option.

The only thing we could guarantee getting on Christmas morning was the satsuma in our stocking, but only because it happened every year. Christmas 1969 was a bit different, as Dad hadn't managed to get our real Christmas tree until the 23rd of December, so we were busy all day on Christmas Eve putting up decorations and adorning this lovely, but spiky, tree. With bedtime looming all was complete and ready for Father Christmas to arrive. We were far too excited to sleep, but despatched to bed anyway.

For a reason only known to him, every year at around 11pm Dad would come up the stairs ringing a bell and doing the whole 'ho, ho, ho' thing. On the face of it, it seems odd as we were supposed to be asleep, but it was Christmas Eve and he knew there was little chance of that. I think ringing the bell was his signal to us that it was our last chance to nod off or there'd be no Santa and no presents. I have no recollection of him filling my stocking, which was hanging on the end of the bottom bunk bed, so I supposed it must have worked.

At 5am we raced downstairs to see if Santa had been. He had, and what a mountain of presents he'd left. As an adult and a parent myself, I understand that a mountain to a small child is really only a moderate pile, but it filled the space between the floor and the bottom branches of the tree.

Where Christmas presents were concerned, we had been brought up to look but not to touch. That was something that resonated with me and Stephen, particularly after the terrible 'cravat episode'.

I suppose, because Dad enjoyed the element of surprise as the present giver, I've never had any desire to know what present I'm getting until I get it. Stephen, however, was different. He took after Mum in his desire to know what was coming his way.

It was three weeks before Christmas 1968, and Mum had popped out to collect Christopher from nursery school. Dad was at work, so this was Stephen's opportunity and he might not get another. We were only left alone for about ten minutes but it only took Stephen half that time to persuade me that it was a good idea to do a Christmas-present hunt. I wasn't keen, but he was my older brother and I was young and impressionable.

We'd wasted half the time, so there wasn't long. Stephen decided that we should split up, so we could search the rooms in the house twice as quickly. We looked under things, in things, on things until, wrapped in a brown paper bag in a kitchen cupboard, Stephen stumbled on two identical pink cravats.

These turned out to be Christopher's Christmas presents to each of us. We quickly inspected the identical pink cravats, each with a gold ring sewn onto one side. It was clear that they had been made for the young gentleman about town who hadn't quite learned to tie a cravat properly, as the other half could be passed through the ring to hold the sides together. Once inspected they went back into the bag and were returned to the cupboard. Nobody was any the wiser.

This little escapade wasn't mentioned in the run-up to Christmas Day. We'd committed the perfect crime and escaped scot-free. However, as soon as I received my present from Christopher, Dad was aware that the excitement level wasn't what it should have been.

I was an honest boy and couldn't help but confess to our little discovery. That wasn't something I needed to do because Dad had already guessed we'd looked at our presents and he wasn't best pleased. It was fair to say that after the dressing-down we both got over this incident it was never going to happen again.

To add insult to injury, that same day Stephen received a Kodak Instamatic camera from Father Christmas so there is photographic evidence of us both wearing our gorgeously patterned pink cravats, gold ring and all. Fortunately it is only in black-and-white; street credibility preserved, I hope.

We'd learned our lesson, so Christmas 1969 involved

plenty of looking at wrapped presents and guessing what might be inside but definitely no touching. After about an hour, we had identified what looked like our main presents and thoroughly discussed what each thought the other was getting. Well, Stephen and Christopher had identified theirs but mine wasn't anywhere to be seen.

That didn't disturb me; I had great confidence that Father Christmas hadn't forgotten to leave my main present and it must be somewhere else. We stared at the pile for a bit longer before all three of us decided it was time to get the present opening started. We weren't daft, though; we'd been here before, so we carefully and quietly crept up the stairs and stood outside our parent's bedroom door.

An ear from each head was pressed firmly to the door to see if there was any sign of movement, but there was only regular breathing and the occasional snort. A quiet knock on the door led to no change in the situation, so the only option to get the day going was to burst through the door.

Dad didn't immediately seem particularly full of Christmas spirit, but once he'd had a good stretch and a yawn he seemed much more amenable to our suggestion that it was time to start Christmas Day and the great present unwrap. He needed to get ready, so instructed us to go downstairs and wait at the table for Mum to serve breakfast, after which he promised we could start.

We adhered to this instruction to the letter, as we

knew Dad was the present distributor. He joined us at the table for his morning cup of coffee. How could someone take so long to drink a mug of coffee? We were ready! Eventually he said we could go into the lounge and get ready, he wouldn't be long.

He was right; it wasn't long before he entered the lounge with the first present in his hand. Every present had a clue Sellotaped to it, written and read out loud by Dad, who absolutely loved them. He spent quite a long time every year getting each clue just right for each present. As we grew up the clues got harder, although always in a very disproportionate way because there were many times we felt the clues had been aimed at someone older.

To Dad, the clue was all-important, sometimes more important than the actual present. Once he'd read it and handed over the present, we were never allowed to guess what was wrapped up inside; we had to try and solve the clue first. Sometimes it took several minutes to decipher something that would have troubled the codebreakers at GCHQ for days before we were told, 'OK, that's close enough,' and we could start unwrapping. At the time, I didn't realise that having to decipher the clues meant that present opening often lasted almost until lunchtime.

It was dragged out more by including the all-important breaks for Mum to get lunch on the go. The way the day panned out was clue-solving and present opening in the morning, a break for lunch, then playing with our new gifts all afternoon. Day sorted.

We had managed to go via the smaller presents from Mum and Dad (aka Father Christmas) and the ones from family, before finally getting to the last act – the big present. Once we reached this point, there were only two presents left under the tree. Dad picked out Christopher's first and he was over the moon with his Meccano set. One down and only one under the tree to go.

Dad picked up a box-shaped present very carefully and read out the clue before handing it to Stephen. It took my brother ages to understand the clue but, with some fairly heavy prompting from our parents, he became aware that Louis Pasteur was a famous chemist. This was the quality clue that led him to his chemistry set.

That was it; there were no more presents left to unwrap. What was happening? Was my main present still zooming around the globe on the back of Father Christmas's sleigh, or had it been left with another child by mistake?

Hang on a minute, though. Dad hadn't given us the usual, 'Well, that's another year done and dusted.' That was the signal that we'd got all that we were getting and it was almost time for lunch.

I didn't understand. There were no presents left, but proceedings hadn't finished. Then I noticed Dad lean towards our heavily decorated tree – we'd made far too many toilet-roll snowmen – and reach for a well-concealed white envelope. I watched, captivated, as he delicately extricated it from the tree. He took far too much time looking at the front before saying, 'Well, that's very odd. It says that it's for Nicholas Hamilton.'

He seemed mystified and I was definitely mystified. You certainly couldn't get a big main present inside an envelope, so why had someone left a letter for me on the Christmas tree?

This was now taking the whole of my attention. I forgot that I was the only one who didn't have a main present and watched transfixed as the letter winged its way in my direction. I looked at the front. My name was typed, so there was no clue there as to who it was from. I opened it.

It was the easiest clue I ever received because all it said was 'Follow the string'. I was confused. I looked up at Dad who was standing in front of me, pleased as punch, pointing towards the lounge door. True enough, once I'd spun round, I saw a bow neatly tied around the door handle. I leapt up and went to investigate. The last time I was this inquisitive, I'd ended up shocked and lying on the floor with a knife in my hand. Was this going to end up the same way?

It wasn't string but wool that had been wrapped around the handle twice, with one end tied in a bow and the other disappearing into the dining room. I was told to unfasten the bow and wrap up the wool as I went. Winding furiously, family in tow, I didn't notice that Dad had stayed behind in the lounge.

Still winding like a boy possessed, I followed the wool

round the dining room and into the kitchen, although unravelling it from around the handles of the cooking pots slowed my progress. Once the pans were done, I headed into the garden, up the path, over the climbing frame and into the shed. From there the wool took me into the outside toilet and everyone else followed. Once untied from the pull-flush chain, I squeezed past Mum and both my brothers and off back towards the house again, through the kitchen, into the dining room and up the stairs.

The ball of wool had started to get rather large. I followed it into our bedroom, out of our bedroom, in and out of the bathroom and into Mum and Dad's bedroom. Back out and back down the stairs and back to where we had started, the lounge. Around the lounge once (Dad had disappeared), into the dining room and the kitchen, out into the garden, the shed and the toilet. Then I was back in the kitchen, through the dining room and back up the stairs. I'm not sure what was harder, racing around or having to wind and carry what was now an enormous ball of wool.

I went back into our bedroom, over the bunk bed and in and out of Mum and Dad's bedroom. I hadn't realised at the time, but Mum had stopped Stephen and Christopher following as I entered the bathroom for a second time. There, standing in the bath was my brand new, second-hand, red bike.

Suddenly Dad appeared to help me lift it out and carry it down the stairs. I can't put into words how excited I was. And, as if that were not enough for anyone, it came with a bag hanging from the back of the saddle. The saddle bag elevated this two-wheeler from an ordinary bike; this bike was posh. Rosa would be so proud!

There have been a few things that Dad did in his life that bemused me, but this one sits at the top of the list. I've tried and tried to work out his thought process, which must have started with the purchase of the bike, via a ton of wool through to a bike in the bath. It was bonkers and I still can't understand how he managed it all.

I can see that the downstairs wool was wrapped around the house while we sat patiently waiting in the lounge for him to finish his coffee, but we'd watched him enter the lounge. He must have cajoled Mum into helping with his cunning plan, because she had to be the one that tied the end of the wool to the handle as she returned from her last kitchen trip to check on the turkey.

I could see that he could get round the house a second time while I was back outside, if he moved quickly enough, but how an earth did he get the bike in the bath without me seeing? I'd been into every room on my first trip round and I definitely didn't spot it in any of them.

The reason for recounting this personal and emotional story is that it shows what lengths Dad went to in order to do the best he could. It may have been a wacky plan, but my excitement grew with every passing minute until I achieved my goal, at which point I was fit to burst.

These were the lengths he went to many times in his life, often at his own cost, to make sure the viewers of BBC2's *Gardeners' World* always got the very best. The only worrying part of this story was that, in order to get to the end result, he was prepared to leave his middle son thinking for nearly six hours that Father Christmas had forgotten him. But on the day, I got a brand new, second-hand, red bike with a saddle bag, so what else was there to worry about?

Chapter 10

I was now free, free to cycle to the woods, free to cycle to my friends, free to cycle anywhere I wanted, and my testicles were also free, free from bruising. What a great invention pneumatic tyres were.

This new-found cycling freedom enabled me to travel the couple of miles to Cheshunt and the training ground of the mighty Tottenham Hotspur. We were used to seeing the players from the 1960s football team around and about our area, as most of them lived in the posher parts of Broxbourne, obviously near to Rosa and Cyril. Dad wasn't a fanatical fan of football, but he was a part-time follower of the ups and downs of our local big team, Tottenham Hotspur (although Broxbourne Badgers F.C. ran them pretty close). He was particularly a fan of their manager Bill Nicholson and the exciting way he had them playing but, although bred in Broxbourne, Dad wasn't born there. This quite plainly explains the reason why he was only a part-time follower, because when you're born in this area everyone knows that you're born with the Spurs cockerel already tattooed on your bottom.

As we only lived ten miles from the ground, it was surprising that we didn't get to go to a match at White Hart Lane. Instead, Dad waited until we'd moved eighty-five miles away before he got round to taking all three of us to a match.

When knocking the ball around in the park with his three children, all under the age of ten, Dad was useful with the ball at his feet but definitely no Pelé. His sporting aspirations were not as a footballer as his passion was for rowing, particularly the single scull. This meant that, when he wasn't spending the weekend working, we would be despatched with him to the Broxbourne Rowing Club.

I loved it down there because, in those days, the surrounding areas were mostly undeveloped and therefore ripe for exploration. With my two brothers also taking part in these escapades, we could quite easily have been starring in the movie *Indiana Jones and the Rowing Club*. Not quite *Indiana Jones and the Temple of Doom*, I grant you, and unsurprising that this script was never considered for the franchise, but all the same we were expert explorers and adventurers. There were sheds and rickety old buildings to explore, as well as fields with crops, much taller than us, to wade through. The boggy ground and tall, treelike and coarse-leaved plants made it feel like a rainforest. We were on the hunt for something – anything. Although not quite sure what it was, we were confident that when we found it we would know that this was it.

Dad would go off rowing, knowing that there were always other adults around if we needed them. These explorations kept us busy for a couple of years until we'd scoured every inch and realised that the thing we were hunting wasn't actually there. If it had been, we'd have found it by now. It was Dad who had instigated the hunt, two years previously, and now he had to find something else to keep three active boys occupied, leaving him free to go about his rowing-club business. As all three of us could swim very well, he came up with a completely ridiculous plan.

I have no idea what was going through his mind at the time, or at any other time throughout his life if I'm honest, but he had spotted a dinghy that wasn't being used. This little brown boat would be perfect for keeping us occupied and, when he told us that we could use it for rowing around on the river, we found it difficult to contain our excitement. The only stipulation was that we never rowed out of sight of the clubhouse.

It was about twenty yards from one bank to the other, so we could now extend our adventures across the water. Off Dad went to get the boat and bring it down to the river. We were trembling with excitement as he appeared out of the boathouse – until I spotted a ray of light piecing through the bottom of the boat. It had a hole.

When he reached the boat-launching ramp, I questioned the slight damage to our new vessel, which could severely scupper our exploration plans. Dad admitted that there had been a bit of an accident and the boat had been speared by the ball at the end of one of the sculling boats, but he said that it was still useable. Our disappointment at the sight of a golf-ball sized hole right in the middle of the of the underside was quickly alleviated, because Dad had already formulated his ridiculous plan.

I look back at a lot of these moments and worry about how many of Dad's genes I might have inherited because, no matter how long you look at his plans and how finely you dissect them, there is no reasoning to be found. Anyway, back to the plan. He explained it in great detail as he always did, and we fell for it hook, line and sinker. As we always did. It wasn't what we had been told that got us excited, it was the enthusiastic manner in which it was delivered. His enthusiasm was something that would hold him in good stead later in his television life.

The plan. Well, the main part was that all three of us should get into the boat and take it in turns to row as far as we could towards the other bank. The jobs were distributed: there would be one rowing, while the other two bailed out as the River Lea gushed in through the hole. We weren't given buckets for this task, we had to use our cupped hands because he'd already worked out that we would need all our hands for the next part of the plan.

When the inevitable happened and the boat sank beneath us, all three of us could then pull it back to the bank. This was achieved by one grabbing the front while two were at the back, all hands on the boat and our legs kicking like fury under the water. During the whole of this operation the boat remained submerged.

Once we got to the bank, we dragged it out of the river, tipped it on its side to empty out the water before pushing it back into the river and starting all over again, only this time with a different rower. What a fantastic plan.

This newfound activity kept us happy for weeks, but eventually the inevitable happened and the excitement waned. We could no longer see the joy in rowing a boat with a hole in it as far and as fast as we could until it sank, then manhandling it back to the bank.

Without a moment to think, Dad's reply was confident and assured. 'I'm not surprised,' he started. 'It's because you're not doing it properly.' We quickly found out what 'properly' meant. According to Dad's explanation, 'properly' meant that we should still row the boat as far as we could before, bailing out the water as we went. Then once water had half-filled the boat and it began to sink, we should all stand up, face the boathouse, salute and sing the national anthem.

A second lease of life had just been discovered. This new format kept us – and everyone else at the rowing club – amused throughout the rest of that summer. Quite often, while facing the boathouse and belting out our song, we had people standing on the bank applauding (together with the occasional pointer and giggler), although no one ever joined in with our rendition of 'God Save the Queen'.

This fun would have continued through the next summer too, if someone hadn't disposed of the dinghy, thinking it had no use with a hole in the bottom. No vision, that's the trouble with some people!

Although Dad had great success keeping his children occupied at the rowing club, it wasn't all plain sailing. The evening of the Annual Broxbourne Rowing Club Social was fast approaching and this was a 'must-go-to' event for Dad. He had Great-grandma Ali confirmed as chief babysitter, Mum had made a suitable dress to wear and Dad had picked up his hired dinner suit for this black-tie event. All was set.

Then, on the very morning of the social, Dad received the devastating news from Rosa that Ali had retired to bed with the flu. In a bit of a panic, he asked his mother if she or Cyril could step in, but they had the mayor and mayoress coming round for a meal, which obviously couldn't be cancelled.

It was late in the day and Dad had no other option left: he and Mum would have to take their children too. This meant their evening would be cut short, but at least they could enjoy part of the event and Dad would get some return on the suit he had hired. It was summer, so the light would be good well into the evening, and there were likely to be others in the same boat so children for us to play with.

When we arrived at the rowing club, there were no other children there. Our parents were dressed in their finery while we were in play clothes, an odd combination but this was an odd situation.

We were told to sit quietly in the corner and provided with a soft drink. Mine was a tomato juice; you couldn't go wrong with a tomato juice, particularly at a posh do. Not that I'd been to a posh do before; the poshest one I'd been to was a friend's birthday party at their house, which was posh because it had a swimming pool.

My drink didn't last long, and neither did those of my brothers, so it wasn't long before we were amusing ourselves by running around people, generally getting in the way. Soon we were sat firmly back in our seats and given a drink and a bag of crisps each, tomato juice and salt and vinegar for me.

How long were these going to keep us quiet? Not very, was the answer. Once they had been consumed, my toes began to twitch. This feeling moved into my feet and then my legs. I slid off my seat and, followed by my brothers, began crawling in, out and around long legs.

We spent the next fifteen minutes generally causing a nuisance before Dad intervened. I'm not sure why because we were doing as we'd been told; I specifically remembered being told not to run around but he never mentioned crawling.

This was the last straw and we were banished outside. It was a lovely, warm summer's evening and the light was good. He told us to occupy ourselves as we normally would during our weekends, but under no circumstances were we to go anywhere near the water.

He was very sure about this because we got the sentence twice, accompanied by a wagging index finger.

We stuck rigidly to the instructions for a good hour, then my curiosity got the better of me. I had started to fish, very unsuccessfully, from the bank of the river on the rowing-club side. I was sure that the reason I never caught any fish wasn't down to my lack of skill but because of a lack of daytime fish. I wondered whether there were more in the river in the evening. This meant a look into the water, something I was confident I could do without falling in. What could go wrong?

The first of my minor errors was the decision to select the concrete boat-launching ramp as the point to look for fish. As I approached, I spotted this green stuff all over the half of the ramp closest to the water. I was curious. It looked like grass from a distance but, even at that tender age and as the son of a landscape gardener, I knew grass didn't grow in concrete. I needed to explore this further.

I hadn't forgotten the finger-wagging and the double instruction given by Dad but decided that, if I was careful, everything would be all right. As I approached I realised that it wasn't grass at all but the green stuff that we found, usually on very wet things, when we were exploring. My mind returned to my original quest.

Slowly and carefully, I edged closer to the water until I approached the fabulous emerald-green carpet covering the end of the ramp. As I placed my foot onto it, it squelched. Unperturbed, I took a second step. That was the final mistake because, as my foot pressed onto the green carpet, it moved.

What happened next came as a bit of a shock. I shot forward as if hurtling across an ice rink and headed straight for the water. I must have looked like a professional skater, as I hurtled across the ramp, still upright, arms out for balance and fell off the end.

As the ramp's trajectory was downwards, it wasn't long before my feet, followed by the rest of me, were submerged. I didn't panic – I was a good swimmer, after all. But the thing is, I didn't try to swim. I just went completely rigid, probably from shock.

Then I saw it: a fish in the water, swimming right in front of me. Then another and another. There were loads of fish in the river. Question answered.

Fortunately Stephen saw my elegant entry into the River Lea. He was quick off the mark and, before I fully entered the water, ran back into the rowing club to get Dad.

I didn't actually see exactly what happened next because I was still slowly sinking to the bottom of the river, but Dad must have sprinted out of the clubhouse and dived full length into the river. Before my feet hit the bottom, he grabbed my collar and my plummet was reversed.

My ascent was rapid. When I broke the surface of the water, all I could see through my spluttering was a dinner suit bobbing next to me with Dad inside it. I was heaved up and out of the water, plonked onto the bank before Dad hauled himself out. Not an easy thing to do with long, sodden tails hanging off your jacket.

Nothing was said. He picked me up and took me to the club changing room where he found an old Broxbourne Rowing Club rugby-style shirt. My beautifully fitting clothing was removed and replaced by this very baggy, ill-fitting shirt. Still without a word being spoken, I was carried back to the clubhouse and placed in a corner. My brothers had their fun outside cut short by my aquatic adventure and joined me in the corner.

Dad continued socialising for a while longer before we were collected and taken home. All the way home, Dad didn't utter a word. In we went and straight off to bed – it was late.

Now, fifty years later, I can only think that the silence was due to his apprehension at returning his hired suit and having to explain to the poor chap behind the counter why the clean suit he had collected just a couple of days earlier now smelled badly of river water. Needless to say, we were never taken to the Broxbourne Rowing Club social evening again.

It wasn't long after this episode that I conceded that there were, in fact, enough fish in the river, so it was just down to me to perfect my fishing technique. This time, however, rather than attempting to grab the fish manually, I decided sitting on the bank with a rod and line was by far the better method and the one that got you into the least trouble.

During many of our weekend trips to the rowing club

in the past I'd been fascinated by the men and boys who sat on the bank and regularly pulled out fish from the water. They all seemed to have rods that were of a much better standard than the one I'd been given by a friend of Dad's, whose child had upgraded. It was obvious that to catch fish I needed new and better equipment. I needed a new rod. Unfortunately my birthday was long gone, but Christmas was on the horizon so I put my request in with Father Christmas for a fishing rod.

You really couldn't imagine my joy when I was handed a thin, but very long, present. There it was, neatly held in bright packaging that consisted of a cardboard backing completely covered with a picture of a man in full fishing gear looking more like a fisherman than any fisherman on the bank of the River Lea. The rod and reel were separate, and all was held onto the cardboard by moulded plastic. I stayed on the floor, my still-packed fishing rod and reel in front of me, just staring at it. I couldn't believe my eyes: a professional fishing rod. I knew it was a top-quality rod and as professional as professional could get in 1968 because it was made of fibreglass.

Being only six, and fishing from the bank at the rowing club, I didn't know about fishing licences, and I'm sure Dad didn't know either because he never mentioned them, so I continued in blissful ignorance of my criminal activity. The two-piece rod was assembled, according to the fairly simple instructions – push one end into the other, then attach the reel. I threaded the line through the hoops, slid on a float and, using my skills as a Cub Scout badge holder for 'knots', carefully tied my hook to the end of the six-pound line. Being an optimistic boy, I went for a reasonably strong line because I was certain that it wouldn't be long before I caught an enormous, weighty fish.

To this hook I attached the necessary fish food in order to tempt that massive fish lurking in the water below. I tried various culinary fishy delights, starting with maggots before moving onto dug-up and hooked-on earthworms, carefully attached bread (which always fell off after getting wet) and even made a mix that my friend's dad said never failed to attract fish to his hook.

I sat there for at least three hours every Saturday and Sunday, rod in hand, while Dad went out rowing in his sculling boat. On his return he always asked me how I was getting on and if I'd caught anything. Every time my answer was that, although I'd had a good day on the bank, I still had nothing to show for my endeavours.

One particular Saturday, when asked, my reply was more negative; I hadn't caught anything and I hadn't had a good day. Dad was taken aback. I was generally a happy easy-going child with a positive outlook. I didn't lose interest quickly and certainly wasn't easily bored.

As Dad was to find out, the reason I hadn't had a good day was that there was a chap sitting on the bank directly opposite me, also fishing. It was quite plain to see that he was a rank amateur; his equipment consisted of a bamboo cane for a rod with a piece of sting tied to one end. At the other end of the string was a bent nail, which he used as a hook. To complete this extraordinarily amateur approach to fishing, he had a dandelion flower tied to his string for a float. Even his tattered, floppy beige hat perched on the top of his head was completely devoid of even a single piece of fishing tackle.

I explained all this to Dad and fully expected a response that would confirm the man's amateur status. Instead he laughed and asked if he'd caught any fish with his cane, string and bent nail. I hesitated because I didn't want to admit that the man was catching at least one fish every ten minutes, while my fish count was still zero. Dad laughed again, but this time for a lot longer.

I started to question him about my equipment. I had the top-notch stuff and was fishless; the man opposite was very successful and fishing in the same bit of river, so it must be down to the equipment.

Dad questioned my technique. The first time I went fishing he had shown me how to cast out my line and what to do if and when I caught a fish. He decided that another lesson was probably due and picked up the rod. What followed scarred me for the rest of my life.

He said, 'This is how you do it, just watch and learn.' In one fluid movement the rod went slowly backwards then came hurtling forwards as the hook, float and line shot out from the end of the rod and into the middle of the river. This was followed by another brief explanation of the technique before he suggested that I had a go and he could critique my technique.

He reeled in the line with the intention of passing it to me. As he lifted the rod, hanging from the hook was a fish. Admittedly it was only a small fish, but it was a FISH! Dad hadn't been sitting on the bank for hours on end and there wasn't any bait attached to the hook. How an earth had he done that?

As calm as you like, all he said was, 'There we are, that's how you do it,' and walked off. If I'd known any expletives at that age, I'm sure I'd have uttered one. Instead I just stood there gobsmacked.

The one thing I did grasp, from what I subsequently realised was a complete fluke, was that if Dad could do it then so could I. I took back ownership of that rod, cast out again, sat down and waited. I waited and waited until Dad called me to go home.

This cycle of events on the bank continued until we moved to Northamptonshire, and even continued there until the momentous day I caught a fish. It was a roach and not a small one at that. This reinspired me. I upgraded my rod a couple of times and even invested in a wicker basket to store my various bits of fishing paraphernalia.

By the age of seventeen, I had added to my haul with two tench and one bream. That's four fish in an eleven-year career as an amateur coarse fisherman. At some point during those eleven years you would have thought that I'd have got the message that fishing probably wasn't the best hobby for me.

I eventually sold up to my best friend's uncle. When I recount this story, people laugh at my meagre haul of four in more than a decade of effort, but I now see that this ingrained perseverance has stood me in good stead during my life in horticulture.

I think Dad's next plan for me was as a direct result of my fishing experience. In order to break the predictability of my days on the bank, he put me forward as a potential cox for the eight. My size meant I was perfect to sit at the end of a rowing boat containing eight burly men, each attached to one end of an oar, while the other end went in and out of the water.

At age seven I wasn't a proficient driver. I think Dad had forgotten that the best I could do was steer a bike, but to do that you just turn the solid handlebar. Without thinking of the consequences, I agreed.

I'd been brought up to try things, but this was different. Basically, I was in charge of the boat's direction. It really didn't matter what any of those eight men did, the path it took was in my tiny hands. Not only that but, when I got into the boat for the first time, I realised that controlling the route the boat took was achieved with two lengths of thin rope, one either side of where I was sitting. I was shown how to grip onto the toggle at each end of those two ropes and informed that the other ends were attached to each side of the rudder that controlled the boat's direction. A nice and easy explanation.

What eight burly men and my dad failed to understand

was that to me this rope and toggle contraption was nothing like a bike. The control method was behind me and therefore operated in the opposite way to a set of handlebars. Even so, I nodded each time I was asked if I understood.

Then came my final set of instructions. These were probably the simplest of all – just keep the boat in the middle of the river. If the boat started going to the right, then pull on the left toggle, and if it started to go the left, pull on the right toggle. Although completely confused and thoroughly out of my depth, I did the Hamilton thing and pretended that I fully understood.

My enthusiasm stemmed totally from a desire to be like my dad. He rowed, albeit in a boat on his own, but this meant that I would be part of the rowing crew. If I got it right, there was a good chance that I could work my way up the rowing ladder until I was sculling alongside him in a boat of my own.

There was no wind at all and the river was like a millpond but, as I climbed gingerly into the boat, it wobbled. These boats are very narrow and it seemed very easy to tip and sink it. The one thing that terrified me the most was not crashing but sinking the boat. I really didn't want to have to perform the national anthem while saluting in front of these eight men.

Once I was in and secure in my seat, I was followed by the eight rowers who seemed to access their seats without any great problem. With a few encouraging words from Dad, we set off. This was my big moment:

it was my time to show that those Hamilton rowing genes had been passed down to me.

What a start! If I'd choreographed those first twenty-five yards up the River Lea it couldn't have gone any better. Dad watched with great pride as we began to speed up and headed towards the first bend in the river. Confident that all was going according to plan, he turned away to head off for a very satisfying half a pint of bitter in the clubhouse.

His timing was always spot on because no sooner had he turned his back than things began to go horribly wrong. Going straight was easy, but turning a corner was a little more complicated. Even if he'd written a large 'L' and 'R' on each of my hands, I still don't think we'd have got round the bend.

As we crashed into the right-hand bank, I saw eight burly men looking in disbelief in my direction. It was blindingly obvious that the only things 'going round the bend', or any bend come to that, on that day were these eight men.

There was no damage done to the boat on this occasion or the next three times we hit the bank; the only damage was to my rowing aspirations. Unsurprisingly, there was no mention again of me coxing an eight or even the reduced boat of four. It was quite plain for everyone to see that the rowing genes were definitely not the right genes for me.

Although he never showed it I'm sure my complete inability to steer a boat was a disappointment because

Dad wasn't just an enthusiastic rower, he was blooming good at it too. In fact he was so enthusiastic that when a rowing colleague told him about the Boston Marathon, he felt that entering this was his next rung up the ladder to rowing greatness. He'd not heard of the race before, but it didn't take long to find out when and where it took place and what was involved.

It was quite important not to get this confused with the Boston Marathon held in Massachusetts held every April, as this one was held in Boston, Lincolnshire. This Boston Marathon was 3,242 miles away from the more famous running race and this one was held every year on the third Sunday in September. The race took place on the River Witham, starting in Lincoln and finishing in Boston.

It was called a marathon by someone who obviously thought that if they mentioned the proper distance it might put off most rowers. The Boston Rowing Marathon actually covered a distance of thirty miles, 1,056 yards. On occasion, in order to avoid a weir or two, they also had to get out of their boats, lift them out of the water and carry them overground to the other side before popping them back in and rowing on.

Dad wasn't deterred and signed himself up. This was a distance way beyond anything he'd travelled before in his sculling boat, but he decided that he was fit enough not to have to train too hard or put in any more miles to complete the course. I suppose with a manual job and three active boys he probably was. More importantly, he approached this race with confidence in his ability.

The day of the race finally came and, much to our surprise, became a family outing to deepest Lincolnshire. For me it was a great adventure because we had always travelled south when venturing anywhere and I'd never been north. Obviously, growing up a soft southerner and it being towards the end of September, I needed to be kitted out with a good woolly jumper, coat, hat and gloves if we were to travel into the frozen tundra.

We waited for Dad to reappear, as he'd popped out whilst we were getting ready. There was a hoot from outside the house and we were ushered through the front door. There was the Austin Morris with a long boat and set of oars strapped to his roof rack, with Dad attaching a red rag to the ball at the front of the boat just as he'd done to the one at the back. The boat was about twice as long as the car, so these indicators of the enormous overhang were essential. It was definitely more boat than car. Off we set and, after more than three hours of 'i-spy', we arrived at our destination.

Dad had arranged to meet a friend at the finishing line so that he could leave both us and the car in Boston and head off to Lincoln and the start of the race. He transferred his boat onto his friend's roof rack and off they set.

Mum decided that we should walk along the riverbank so that we could spot him coming from further up the river, then sprint along to the finishing line with him. The finishing line was surrounded by fields so in the meantime we played on the grass and climbed some trees before sitting down to a fabulous picnic. It wasn't long before the competitors finally began to pass us and head towards the finish. I was unaware of the staggered start for the boats; I had only ever seen races where all the competitors started at the same time, so it came as a bit of as shock to me that Dad wasn't the first one pass us and in the lead.

Then it was all about being eagle-eyed to spot Dad. As I found out later, the rowers had set off at two-minute intervals so once they started to pass they came thick and fast. There was the odd gap where a competitor had decided enough was enough, as well as some who passed quite slowly, having been overtaken by several other rowers.

Suddenly there was Dad, quite red in the cheeks but rowing like the clappers. We all shouted, cheered and waved him on and then concentrated on running along the edge of the river while avoiding the enormous cowpats that littered our path. Thinking about it now, injury by cowpat seems a minor concern compared to the torture Dad was enduring. He was still overtaking other rowers in his run up to the line and, as he passed the finishing post, he let go of his oars and collapsed forward, head between his raised knees. His boat was still advancing forward but he didn't move. It was exhaustion like he'd never experienced before.

He had given it his all and he knew that, having passed enough rowers with nobody overtaking him, he must have won. After all the competitors had crossed the finishing line, the totting-up began; the rowers worked out the time they'd taken to complete the course by comparing the time they'd started with the time they finished. It was quite simple and easy to determine the winner. However, it was at this point that the real problems started.

A steward came to Dad to let him know that, although they had his finishing time, nobody had actually logged his starting time. They didn't even know who he had set off after or before. Dad had an approximate starting time, but unfortunately nothing was running to time and the racers were not necessarily starting in the order they were listed as some of them hadn't got to the start line in time. Dad's approximation of his starting time was not precise enough.

Several rowers who were listed as setting off before him were asked if they could confirm that Dad had passed them. All said he had, except for one. Dad was crystal clear in his mind that this chap was the fourth rower he had passed on his epic journey, but this rower had obviously decided that he wanted to win at all costs. The adjudicators made their decision and they awarded the winner's trophy to the other man. Dad was gutted.

He spent some time with the adjudicators, trying to make them see sense and explaining how he must have passed the man crowned as winner, but to no avail. As we silently trudged back towards the car, I noticed Dad's hands were covered in blisters. He had given this race his all and he would never compete in the Boston Marathon again.

I was curious about why this other rower had been awarded the winner's trophy when Dad was so positive that he was the winner. As always Dad was philosophical about it and told me that he knew he came first and so did the man who was awarded first place; if this other man wanted to cheat to win then it was a hollow victory. Dad would always know that he'd won the race and that was all that was important. He proclaimed, 'You don't get anywhere by cheating,' an excellent life lesson for a young boy.

Even witnessing Dad's obvious disappointment that followed this, added to the setback in my short but eventful rowing career, didn't deter me from visiting the rowing club. If anything, it increased my determination to excel at fishing. Not that I ever achieved that goal, but I learned to swim in the river as opposed to using the 'plummeting to the bottom' technique I'd previously employed.

During the summer of 1970 the rowing club committee decided to put on a family event. There would be activities to occupy both adults and children on, in, and out of the water. Thankfully I wasn't asked to participate in any of the boating activities but, much to my astonishment, I discovered that Dad had entered Stephen and me in the swimming race. It was a sprint across the River Lea to the opposite bank and back.

I discovered I was taking part about ten minutes

before the start. I'm pretty sure the reason was a lack of contestants – I was 'volunteered' to bulk up the numbers. As I lined up on the bank with the rest of the male contestants, it was obvious that I was the youngest. The oldest was a fifteen-year-old.

There was a healthy crowd of spectators to cheer on their favourites and family loyalties were much in evidence. Ready for the start, I crouched, arms out to the front, and awaited the instruction to go. Loudly and deliberately the starter shouted, 'Ready, steady, go,' and we were off.

I had no plan as to how to pace the race; even if I'd had more notice I still wouldn't have conceived a plan. It was well known that I was like a bull in a china shop, so my technique was always going to be to swim to the opposite bank and back as fast as my little arms and legs would take me.

As I reached the other side of the river, touched the bank and turned for my return leg, I could see the two oldest boys in the distance hauling themselves out of the river at the starting point. They'd finished already. That just made me more determined. Head down, I swam my best front crawl. Everyone else probably finished before I was halfway back but that meant, for those last few yards, all the cheering from the large crowd was for me. I finished to the biggest roar I've ever experienced and I definitely felt like a winner. Not being an attention-seeker, I hopped out of the river and, rather than acknowledging my adoring public, I disappeared into the big towel Mum was holding out for me.

It wasn't long before the prize-giving started. The winner of the girls' race was awarded her prize and then it was our turn to step forward. The announcer called out the name of the winner, who promptly stepped forward to collect his prize, a book. Just as I was turning away thinking the formalities were finished, I suddenly heard my name being called out.

Stunned, I stopped in my tracks and looked towards the announcer. In an unexpected twist, the committee had decided to award an extra prize to the gallant last-placed swimmer in the boy's race for the most enthusiastic swim. As it was a last-minute decision, they obtained my prize from one of the stalls. Still in a state of shock at being called, I moved forward and was handed my very special prize – a large, pink, plastic tennis racket.

If I'd been older, I might not have appreciated the quality of this prize but, as an exhausted eight-year-old, I was over the moon to have won something. At that age I really wasn't interested in how trendy or exclusive my prize was, and its obvious cheapness never came in to the equation. Although I never used it for tennis or any other sport, I treasured it.

To make my award seem that bit more special, Dad told me it was something that only a very few people owned. Looking back, I now understand that what he actually meant was that it was something that only a few people owned because it was very cheap and very, very pink!

Dad seemed to have an answer for everything and an ability to avoid emotional situations, particularly when tears were shed. From an early age, I realised running was far better than walking. This high-velocity travel was always going to result in tangled legs, trips or an occasional impression of a circus artist who'd been shot from a cannon, all of which invariably ended up with me getting up close and personal with the pavement. That generally resulted in some tears beginning to flow, but Dad always had an answer. In a concerned tone he would say, 'I hope you haven't damaged the pavement because I don't want to get in trouble with the council.'

Immediately there was no more thought of crying; I was up and I was off. It was a great way to divert a distraught child, although his concerned tone was definitely for the potential cost of replacing damaged slabs and not the damaged parts of my body!

His ability to conjure up a line to which there could be no response wasn't restricted to potentially tearful situations. He also applied it if I felt too ill to go to school. This didn't happen often because I really liked going to school. However, if this situation ever arose he started with a question: 'Can you walk?' Without any thought of lying, I always told the truth and replied that I could. This reply led him to conclude: 'Well, if you can walk, you're well enough to go to school, so get dressed.'

Some may feel that this method of parenting is rather harsh but that's certainly not the way I see it. The 'if you can walk' statement has had a massive impact on my life. I don't see illness as a barrier to doing what I need to do and I can count on one hand the number of days I've had off work for what a doctor would class as a minor illness.

Chapter 11

For the first five years of my life, our main family summer holiday consisted of camping in a field. It was Dad who was the driving force in this decision, having been one of the two youngest-ever Queen Scouts in his day (the other was his twin brother, Tony).

We had these holidays when he could take a week away from his landscaping work. The great benefit of camping in the 1960s was that you could do it at short notice; you could always find a camp site or friendly farmer in your preferred location with space for your tent.

Our usual destination was the seaside, generally Cornwall, and our seaside holiday always started about a mile from home. At this point Dad would ask if any of us could see the sea yet. It's a fair question to ask children whose eyesight is perfect – but asking when it's still 285 miles away? He wasn't daft; he knew looking for the sea would keep us quietly scouring the landscape for most the journey.

When our concentration waned, he would move onto his standby game of i-spy. His little eye with which he spied nearly always managed to see something none of us could, so he could keep us thinking and guessing for quite some time.

Our most memorable family camping expedition was when we set up our tent in a field very close to a popular campsite. As usual Dad hadn't pre-booked a site, and this particular year the world and his wife had also decided to spend their summer holiday camping in Cornwall. When we arrived, the campsite we'd planned to use was full.

As we headed off towards another site, Dad noticed a farmer in his field. We screeched to a halt and Dad leapt out and persuaded the farmer to let us to camp in his field. He was so pleased with himself, not because he'd saved the day and his family had a canvas roof over their heads for the night, but because he got the use of the field for half the price of the campsite down the road.

The Austin Morris was packed to the brim with the second-hand, six-person tent Dad had bought a couple of weeks earlier, all our clothing and cooking equipment for the week, as well as Mum and we three boys. Luckily it had a roof rack. As we were now camping in a field all on our own, Dad was able to drive right up to our allocated spot.

He was very pleased with the tent he'd bought. The canvas cover was in one bag, and the tubular metal poles that would form the framework were in another bag. As this tent had had a previous life (and just like the flat-pack furniture we buy these days), there were no instructions. This led to great hilarity and a few very odd combinations as we tried to work out how the poles fitted together. As the tent construction moved into its second hour, the laughter turned into frustration. Eventually, after nearly two hours, Dad completed the task and the tent was ready for the family to move into for our luxury week's holiday.

It wasn't long before the little Campingaz stove was set up and Mum started making the evening meal while Dad sorted out the sleeping arrangements. This luxury tent had internal netting partitions, which made his job considerably less stressful than cooking a family meal on a one-burner stove. Our three-bedroomed tent was set out so that Mum and Dad had one of the back rooms, the other was piled full of clothes and food, and we three boys shared the room next to the doorway.

The tent was great, like a small house, with enough headroom for Dad to stand upright without banging his head. With full stomachs, and very tired after a long journey and the excitement of being on holiday, we settled into our sleeping bags.

The night passed without incident and I slept like a log. That wasn't uncommon for me; what was uncommon was opening my eyes to find a pair of the most enormous nostrils I'd ever seen inches from my own. They were on the end of a long snout above which there was an enormous pair of eyes that were looking straight at me.

I let out a loud shriek. Dad was out of his sleeping bag

and through the gap in his netted partition in seconds, to see what was the cause of this blood-curdling scream. As he leapt into the central living section of the tent, he was confronted by a Friesian cow. Baffled, he turned toward our room where he found me with my head sticking out of the top of my sleeping bag, face as white as a sheet, eyes wide open and staring into the eyes of the aforesaid cow who hadn't moved despite my scream.

To be honest, I was expecting a bit more fatherly action rather than I got. Dad crumpled into a heap, clutching his sides and laughing so much that he started to cry. The cow, satisfied with its inspection of this new construction in her field, meandered off into the sunrise. This was definitely not how I wanted our holiday to start, but even during childhood I was quite stoical and quickly put this trauma behind me. That was fortunate, because there was worse to come.

Dad was a fountain of ideas and that fountain never stopped flowing. He was naturally very enthusiastic, but even more so when an idea came from his own warped brain. He was particularly keen on ideas that would keep us occupied for hours.

Once the trauma of the bovine encounter had passed, we set off for the beach. The sun was shining and there wasn't a cloud in the sky. Off we headed with us three boys gripping our buckets and spades while Mum and Dad staggered behind with the day's supply of food and other essentials. We crossed the field, mountaineered over sand dunes – and there it was: a beautiful long stretch of golden sand, and the sea stretching out to the horizon.

We stopped at the of the dunes to take in the view, and Dad suggested a race into the sea. He not only had the longest (and thinnest) legs but he also knew how to run down a sand dune. He dropped the bags he was carrying and lolloped off while we three descended with a combination of running, rolling and falling. Fortunately the tide was in, so once he was down Dad ran much more slowly towards the crashing waves. He timed his arrival so that Stephen and I overtook him and Christopher just about caught up with him, then he stopped short of the sea so we could plough into the water.

As Dad was fully aware, the temperature of the water resembled that of the Arctic Sea. When we started jumping up and down and shouting how cold it was, the only reply we got was, 'Don't be such softies!' Eventually our bodies acclimatised to the freezing temperature and we swam and played in the water for well over an hour while Dad lay on his towel, one eye open towards the sea and the other firmly shut, relaxing while he could.

When we finally emerged, teeth chattering and bodies shivering, Mum was there to rub us down with towels while Dad prepared the buckets and spades. He'd obviously decided that building sandcastles was our next task. I wasn't particularly good at this but I gave it my best shot, even though the top of my castles always collapsed. We managed a small town's worth of castles before lunchtime.

Sandwiches consumed and orange juice drunk, we were ready for an afternoon of play. What we hadn't realised was that, while watching us making sandcastles, Dad had noticed all the holes we'd made when filling our buckets. With these in mind, and while chewing on a cheese-and-pickle sandwich, Dad's brain spat out another of his magnificent ideas.

He'd come up with the idea that we boys should combine our efforts and dig the deepest hole that anyone had ever dug. He reckoned that we would know when we'd done this by standing in the hole; as long as the top of it came level with Stephen's shoulders, we would be the new record holders.

During lunch the clouds had rolled in and the sun was nowhere to be seen, so we were glad of something energetic to do to keep ourselves warm. Dad helped us find the perfect spot, far enough from where he and Mum were sitting but close enough to be observed.

We started digging enthusiastically, and it wasn't long before the major flaw in Dad's plan became evident. None of us was particularly tall so digging the hole probably didn't take as long as he had anticipated. Now we'd done it, it was ready for testing and photo taking so that we could claim the record. Dad meandered over to look at our efforts, his brain in overdrive as he tried to think of something else to keep us busy.

By the time he'd walked the six paces from his towel to the edge of our massive hole, he had a plan. He decided that taking a picture of us in the hole was not the best way to go about claiming the record. The best way (Dad's way) was for him to take a picture of us in age order standing next to the hole, and then one with us all *in* the hole. It would then be clear how tall we were and how deep the hole was.

He walked back to get his camera while we lined up, looking as proud as Punch of our achievement. When Dad returned, he took the photo of us next to the hole and then we all jumped into it and stood there. This was where his cunning plan took a rather devilish twist.

According to the expert with the camera, the best way to take the second picture was with the hole filled in. Somewhat confused, I started to climb out but apparently he meant with the hole filled in and the three of us still in it.

We stood like statues in our swimming trunks as Dad grabbed one of our spades and started to fill in the hole. He asked Christopher and me to create a small mound to stand on so that our shoulders were at the same level as Stephen's. He then carefully filled in the gap around us with the damp cold sand we'd only just excavated. Being a landscaper you would expect him to get his levels right, and he was spot on. By the time he'd finished filling in the hole, all our Adam's apples were perfectly level with the top of the sand.

We were very excited as the final spade full of sand was thrown in and Dad smoothed the sand with the back of the spade. We agreed that this was the funniest thing that had ever happened to us. Dad took the picture and then, telling us he'd be back in a minute, retreated to his towel.

After some time, it became apparent that his watch must have stopped. We could see him relaxing full length on his towel, but he must have been just out of earshot because he didn't seem to hear our calls. I don't know how long we were there for because I didn't possess a watch, and even if I had I couldn't have seen it because my arms were pinned to my side by several tons of sand.

Eventually Dad tootled over and dug down deep enough to release our arms, then he left us to finish off the job with our hands. He was so proud of such a successful parenting day.

He tried to use the same ploy the next day, but we weren't going to fall for it again. Instead we spent the second day swimming, building sandcastles with Dad and letting him win at beach cricket.

Dad's choice of holidaying in Cornwall was turning out to be perfect. Nobody could have foreseen how this would change.

After such a great day on the beach, we returned to the cow field where we were encouraged to get the cricket set out for a proper game. It was somewhat difficult when there were cowpats littering the pitch, but we did the best we could. It kept us occupied while Mum rustled up dinner – salad, followed by the classic traditionally English pudding of tinned fruit salad. After we'd played a few rounds of the card game 'old maid', we were packed off to bed.

I'd had a very active day so I fell asleep quickly. Suddenly I was woken by the loudest clap of thunder I'd ever heard. When I opened my eyes, I thought the gaslight had been left on but then it suddenly went completely dark again. Another lightning flash a few seconds later explained all.

I lay in my sleeping bag watching the lightning through the canvas tent roof. It wasn't long before the light show and the thunderclaps were joined by a tap, tap, tapping on the tent roof. The rain started with just a few large drops before rapidly increasing until it was hammering down. There were either large hailstones mixed in with it or the drops were the size of tennis balls because they made a terrific noise on the canvas and the whole tent started to shake.

Dad appeared to reassure us that all was well and that this was just a passing storm. At that moment, I felt a drop of water hit my left ear then a drop on my sleeping bag. Before long, rain was landing on everything in the tent, including us. Mum joined us and asked why the tent was leaking. Dad put this minor problem down to the ferocity of the storm, an explanation we accepted without question.

This torrent seemed to last for ages but eventually I nodded back off to sleep. When I woke in the morning, the thunder and lightning had stopped but the rain hadn't. It wasn't so fierce, but it was falling steadily. Unfortunately it was dripping steadily inside the tent, too.

Eventually the rain stopped, but it reappeared for every one of the remaining four nights of our holiday. Each morning Mum hung up our sleeping bags on the makeshift line that Dad had erected so that they were dry when we got back into them. Our clothes were kept inside the Austin Morris, as this was the only dry place we had. If nothing else, waking up in a soggy sleeping bag made going into the cold sea a pleasure.

Some twenty years later, while reminding Dad of this holiday and comparing it to a very rainy week I'd just spent in the Lake District, I prised a confession from him. With a wry smile he admitted that when he'd bought the tent he hadn't asked if it had been waterproofed. He was embarrassed that he, an ex-Queen Scout, had been so remiss. We'd have had as much protection from the elements if we'd been sleeping under a giant slice of Gruyère cheese.

By the time he remembered that he should have waterproofed it before we left home, we were halfway to Cornwall so he decided on the 'keeping his fingers crossed' method. When his worst fears were realised, he decided not to mention it. In fact, he decided not to mention it for twenty years!

This soggy holiday brought the summer camping trips in Cornwall to an abrupt end and ushered in a new and more exciting burst of holiday fun – we went continental. When we were children, Mum would talk to my brothers and me in French when we were at home, so we were bilingual when we went to school.

Dad's French was sufficient for him to hold a sensible conversation, but only with the use of an occasional English word. He was very much a pidgin French speaker – one wonders why he thought it sensible to marry a French lady whose family didn't speak particularly good English. This led to moments when the in-laws visited that were interesting, sometimes awkward – but always very funny to his children. Fortunately for Dad, visits from his in-laws were a rare occurrence.

As we only lived a stone's throw from Rosa and Cyril they saw us all the time, but it was harder for Mum's parents to see their English grandchildren. Consequently, from the age of six Stephen and I would be packed off to France for the school summer holidays. This was a real treat because we had four older French cousins, so we were well and truly spoiled. Dad was delighted with this arrangement because he was taking part in a French exchange but nobody was coming back to stay with us. The icing on the cake was that our French grandparents not only took care of our upkeep for the whole holiday but they also paid for our flights.

Almost as soon as we finished school, Mum started to pack a suitcase for us and, before the week was out, we were driven to Heathrow Airport. Were they desperate to get rid of us? Neither Stephen nor I had ever flown without at least one parent before, so our first solo trip should have been very daunting for me, but I had an older brother for company so I was fine.

After the usual wait in the departures lounge, we

said our goodbyes before being passed into the capable hands of an air hostess, our guardian for the flight. Once the handover was completed, our lives improved dramatically and we were pampered to within an inch of our lives. We got anything – yes, anything – we wanted. This was such a contrast to home. We consumed as many sweets as we could, drank copious amounts of squash and ate all the food that was put in front of us. It was even better than an all-you-can-eat buffet, because we just said yes and the food appeared. We didn't even have to get it ourselves.

Such a fantastic journey could easily have over-shadowed the holiday itself, but our grandparents would never allow that to happen. When we landed at Orly Airport we were met by Mamé and Pépère. They were typical of their generation and expected to be revered by their grandchildren. They lived in a third-floor-flat in the Paris *département* of Saint-Mandé and we always chose to travel in the *ascenseur*. This lift was surrounded by ornate open ironwork so we could see the gap around the floor, and it had manually operated double doors. Being able to see all around the lift gave us the impression that we were floating up to the third floor, which was scary and exciting in equal parts – *fantastique*!

Stephen and I slept in the same double bed, which had the weirdest pillows I'd ever seen. I've never been able to get on with the French sausage-shaped pillow! We were woken every morning by a puffing noise outside our bedroom door that moved up and down the corridor. The first time we heard it, I couldn't help having a sneaky peak through the crack in the slightly open door.

In hindsight, it was not the sort of thing I would choose to witness at that ungodly hour of the morning. There was my grandfather trotting up and down the narrow hallway in his string vest and pants, puffing out heavily as he went. Pépère had fought with the Free French during the war and still liked to do his early-morning exercises. The white hairs on his chest were bursting out of the top of his vest as he lifted his knees as high as he could on every second trip up the corridor. This may well be the reason I grew up determined never to go jogging.

I developed a weird addiction to peering through the gap to witness Pépère's exercise regime. In the end, it went from being the worst to the funniest start to the day.

Once the morning's excitement was over, it was time for the most important part of any French person's day – food. I love food: French cheese, anything with garlic in it, baguettes (proper French ones, obviously) and anything produced by French cooks, such as Mum or Mamé. I can't imagine how you could start the day better than with a panting septuagenarian followed by a bowl of hot chocolate and a warm croissant or two.

Breakfast was fairly swiftly followed by elevenses, then lunch, which in turn was followed by an afternoon snack and then dinner. Nothing else mattered as long as we were in place at every meal time. I have to admit that I was like a pig in its own recyclable product.

Although Paris is a beautiful city with plenty of green spaces to keep two young boys occupied, after a couple of days we were bundled into our grandparents' big old Citroen and whisked off to an aunt's house in the country. Mum had three sisters: Monique and Micheline who were older, and Claude who was younger.

We generally went to Micheline and her husband Pierre's house just outside Paris. This was a typical French country home with beautiful old shutters on every window and a large garden. The surrounding country roads and fields were perfect for cycling and exploring with our older cousins, Eric and Christian. Eric was ten years older than me, so I looked up to him and took his word as gospel. There were only two bicycles, which was a problem, so Eric and Christian rode them and we sat on the handlebars. It was here that my daredevil streak emerged and we discovered one of my favourite activities.

When Eric decided on anything, I always agreed. On one trip around the country roads when I was perched on his handlebars, we stopped at the top of a rather steep hill that ended at a T-junction. Beyond was a field of maize. Eric thought it would be fun to hurtle down the hill as fast as possible, across the road at the bottom and see how far we could get into the field. I thought this was an excellent idea; what I hadn't realised was that he had included me in his master plan.

Off we set. Eric pedalled like fury and the bike reached a speed I've never achieved since, on or in a piece of non-motorised machinery. The velocity and G-force were so great that the wind wasn't so much blowing through my hair as ripping it out by the roots. I gripped the handlebars as if my life depended on it, as it unquestionably did.

We flew across the T-junction and hit the grass verge on the other side of the road so hard that we were both ejected from our seats. I was in front so I went first but, being bigger and heavier, Eric soon flew past me. It wasn't a controlled flight and the maize definitely made the landing a lot softer and safer than it could have been.

Still at the top of the hill, Christian and Stephen decided that Eric's plan was not as good as it had sounded initially and came down the hill at a more reasonable pace. Removing bits of maize, I rose from the ground and waited to see where Eric had landed. By the time we got back to the road, Christian had retrieved our bike from the field and was removing maize cobs from between its spokes. Eric, a bit battered and bruised, got back into the saddle. I climbed back on the handlebars – and asked if we could do it again! Unfortunately Eric became all health and safety and refused. I was gutted.

The following summer, we went with Mamé and Pépère to stay with my great-grandparents in Romorantin-Lanthenay, about 130 miles south of Paris. As the roads were clear, we arrived sooner than expected. As we alighted from the Citroën, my great-grandmother burst out of the house in a bit of a flap with her wig on back to front. I giggled as quietly as I could.

Our other holiday destination was Mum's sister Claude's house. She should have been severely reprimanded for marrying her husband Claud instead of having the sense to marry someone with a different name, because it was very confusing for a young Anglo-French boy. They had a holiday home in Hossegor on the south-western coast of France, situated just behind the sand dunes on the edge of a fantastic beach. We played games on the beach and swam in the sea. These were carefree times, made even better because the French don't seem to bury their children up to their chins in sand.

There were occasions when being fluent in French was definitely not an asset. One occurred during a three-week holiday in Corsica. It was a year after my heart operation, so I was twenty years old. The year before, Micheline had offered me a paid-for holiday at her new holiday house in Corsica to recuperate after my surgery. However, Dr Gribbin had flatly refused to allow me to leave the country in case something went wrong. Micheline extended her offer by a year and I flew out in early August 1982.

Her house was up in the hills overlooking the gorgeous Gulf de Sagone. Once I'd settled in, she asked if I fancied windsurfing as she had all the kit for when

Eric and Christian stayed. Bear in mind that my last experience with a vessel used for travelling on water ended in it crashing several times into the bank, so I was rather apprehensive. I was a complete novice, having only seen windsurfing on the television, but Micheline convinced me that I'd love it. She had a learner board, which apparently travelled at the speed of an oil tanker, so off we went.

At the beach, I underwent extensive tuition (which lasted at least two minutes) before the board was plonked into the sea and off I went. As I set off, I knew that Micheline's confidence in my windsurfing abilities was misplaced, but I carried on anyway.

I'd been on the water for about an hour before disaster struck. When I say on the water, I was in it most of the time, but I did master an important element of windsurfing: the art of climbing back onto the board without falling off straight away.

There was a good breeze and it didn't take me long to realise that windsurfing is definitely harder than it looks. Micheline taught me to push the mast and sail away when I fell so that the mast didn't crash down on my head. That seemed like an excellent plan for self-preservation, so I followed her instructions.

Once again I felt myself losing balance, so I vigorously pushed the sail and mast away from me and entered the water feet first on the opposite side of the board. When I emerged from the water, a rather angry lady in a flowery swimming cap was emerging from under my sail. The mast had landed fair and square across her head.

She was not in the swimmers' area but that didn't stop her from ranting at me. I can't remember exactly what she said but it was along the lines of, 'Are you an idiot? Could you not see me swimming? If you can't windsurf properly, you shouldn't be out on the water. Typical inconsiderate child!'

Child? I was twenty! So what did this self-respecting young Anglo-Saxon do? Obviously I replied, 'Sorry, I don't understand – English.' It worked. She swam off having forgotten about me; now she just hated the English in general.

Not disheartened by this slight mishap, I ploughed on. After a couple of days of continual on, off, on, off the board, I was managing to stay on for at least two minutes before having to take a bit of a dip. Micheline had noticed my rapid improvement and said that I should be a bit more adventurous and head out to sea. There was a moderate breeze so, not being one to turn down a challenge, I set off. I ploughed on at a decent rate, standing on my board and feeling proud of my expertise, and I only dipped into the Mediterranean once during the first fifteen minutes. I almost felt like a professional.

By this time the beach was a distant haze. It was also at this point that reality dawned: I was heading off towards Spain with no idea how to turn round. This, I realised, was a major flaw in Micheline's initial intensive beach tuition. I didn't think I'd make the full 341 miles to Barcelona so I needed an alternative plan. All I could think of was to jump off the board and turn it round, so that it was facing the right way to Corsica.

I hopped on and set off back towards the Gulf of Sagone. When I explained the error in her tuition to Micheline, she seemed rather indifferent. I couldn't seem to shift the thought that maybe she'd done it on purpose!

Although Dad was always pleased to have us home, our continental escapades didn't always end favourably. Returning from a family holiday to Hossegor, we were met with an utter disaster.

Dad hadn't been able to come with us due to work commitments. While we were away there had been no need for him to think of anything but getting on with work before the bad weather started. On the face of it, it was the perfect situation for him: work during the day and the rowing club most evenings. However, while the rest of the family was on holiday he did have certain responsibilities, namely the pets. This was not something he relished but a clear indication as to where my appalling memory genes come from…

When we returned home and asked where the guinea pigs were, Dad seemed a bit taken aback. Then he said that they'd escaped. We were soon joined by Pushkin, our cat, who was still alive and still at home. We found the tortoise – eventually; the reason it took so long to find him was that the grass in the back garden was now almost a foot high. It hadn't been cut for the whole six weeks we had been on holiday.

The guinea pig puzzle was something I didn't work out at the time because I wholeheartedly believed Dad's explanation. However, as I reached my teenage years it dawned on me that the guinea pigs had not escaped because this would have been as likely as them escaping from Alcatraz. Dad had constructed a wooden home for them, as well as a chicken-wire-covered run attached to the ground by pegs. As viewers of *Gardeners' World* would later find out, when he built something it was built to last. Escape from the run would have been impossible.

After successfully finding the tortoise, Dad told us that our luck was in and we might find the guinea pigs too if we looked long and hard. Wading through the grass was akin to moving through a tropical rainforest as we hunted high and low in our small garden. We extended our search into the next-door neighbour's garden and to the piece of wasteland opposite, but there was no sign of them.

Eventually Dad announced that they were probably now making a life for themselves in a lovely piece of local countryside and would raise their family there. As a teenager, I was savvy enough to finally understand that he'd obviously forgotten to feed the two guinea pigs and their new countryside home was, in fact, guinea pig heaven.

Chapter 12

In 1970, as the city began to encroach on rural Hertfordshire, Rosa decided it was time she and Cyril escaped London yet again and moved further north. This time their destination was Northamptonshire and a small village called Ashley. They moved to a large bungalow with a large garden, which was definitely on the posh side of the main street. However, it wasn't long before Great-grandma Ali followed them. Much to Rosa's embarrassment, she moved into one of the small council houses on the opposite side of the road.

Rosa never spoke about her East End roots to her new neighbours, preferring to focus on their life from Broxbourne onwards. Ali, as proud as Punch, spoke for her.

It was at this point that Dad started to get disillusioned with landscaping. Many years later he explained to me that he loved the work and didn't mind the hard graft but he loathed the feeling of being a debt collector.

Dad wasn't a perfectionist but he always applied the same principle – if a job's worth doing, then it's worth doing well. This resulted in him often spending too long on a job to ensure it was up to the standard he'd set himself. Consequently he wasn't generating the profit he needed to provide his family with a more comfortable life and we continued to survive on the breadline.

To add insult to injury, most of his work was in North London, an area littered with large houses and homeowners who were not short of a bob or two. Dad always said that the reason they had money was because they didn't like to part with it. All too often, having finished a job, he found himself spending several weeks knocking on the same doors and pleading with the inhabitants to pay him for the excellent job he'd done for them. He hated having to beg for the money he was owed.

This experience certainly didn't put him off horti-culture, just being a self-employed landscaper. He decided that he needed a change. Fortunately Cyril had so much work on that he needed a hand, so Dad went from being a self-employed landscaper/debt collector to being a salesman, another job he really didn't particularly like. As we all saw on *Gardeners' World* he certainly had the 'gift of the gab', but he wasn't a salesman and he knew it. But he knew this was only a short-term position and he had his eyes on a bigger prize. Then something happened that would change all of our lives forever.

Dad travelled from Wormley to Ashley at the beginning of most weeks to meet Cyril and plan their actions for the next five days. Even though he knew he wasn't cut out for this role, Dad approached it with the enthusiasm he approached everything, and he was determined not to let his own father down. It was on one of his many selling trips that he passed a derelict garden centre that was up for sale. It was in Northamptonshire, on Warkton Lane in Kettering, and not too far from Rosa and Cyril in Ashley.

When he'd left landscaping, Dad had hoped to rent a garden centre where he could grow and sell plants, so finding this was like a dream. The problem was that it was a dream he couldn't afford; he certainly didn't have that sort of money to invest, nor did he have credibility with the bank to get a full mortgage. He did, however, have Cyril whose business was thriving. Dad went cap in hand to his dad, a situation most children can relate to!

Cyril wasn't daft; he knew that his middle son wasn't going to spend the rest of his life as a salesman. He knew that Dad's first and only love was horticulture and that maybe this was the section of horticulture that would see him through the rest of his working life. Cyril mustered up the down payment Dad needed in order for the bank to supply the remainder in the form of a small mortgage.

Cyril was clear that although he was lending money to his son, he wanted it doing properly. An agreement was drawn up, which Dad duly signed, stating the amount of the loan and the repayment terms. It wasn't actually a legal document drawn up by a solicitor but one written by Cyril. Dad didn't read it, believing that his own father wouldn't put anything unexpected in it.

A few days later, when he had a moment's peace, Dad picked up the agreement and read on. It said that he was committed to paying the interest on the loan. A few lines of waffle later, it mentioned the amount of the loan. Many lines later, just before the end of the document where it wasn't obvious, it stated that the interest had been set at a constant zero per cent and that the loan was only to be repaid when Dad had made his millions. Cyril obviously didn't understand horticulture. That was one very rare occasion when Dad was lost for words.

The Wharf Road house was on the market and house-hunting had started. It wasn't long before there was an offer for our small, terraced house and soon after my parents found a semi-detached house on a relatively new estate in Kettering. The new house was situated on the corner plot at the end of a row of semi-detached houses in St Saviours Road, only a ten-minute walk from the garden centre.

The garden centre sale went through rapidly as there wasn't a queue of people putting down offers. The estate agent had it listed as 'in need of modernisation', which was as far removed from the truth as possible; it should have been described as derelict. Dad would probably have been wiser to knock down what was left standing and start from scratch, but his finances didn't allow for that. They also didn't allow for much paid help, so he set about this project very much on his own.

The windows were rotten wooden frames, and most were missing their glass. The only door was hanging on one rusty old hinge. There was a large storage shed around the back which had walls – no roof, just walls. Best of all, there was a very rickety, though still standing, wooden framework of a long greenhouse. The outside area was mud. As a nine year old, I couldn't understand how Dad managed to stand on the edge of his kingdom and imagine it finished, open and selling.

The first job was to get an income flow, so the priority was to get the shop up and running. I was on hand to remove windows and doors because, even at that young age, I found I could easily push them out and onto the floor. Then it was on to the roof, then the walls and finally the floor. Next Dad moved on to the outside of the building. He removed the flaky paint and sealed the bricks prior to rendering them. Rendering was a great process; he filled a contraption that he'd hired with white stuff, pointed the machine towards the wall and turned the handle clockwise like a maniac. The goo in the machine stuck to the wall like magic; it resembled the Polyfilla that some of Rosa's friends used to try and disguise the fact that they were now grandparents.

I was desperate to have a go on this machine; after much pestering I got my chance and rendered about one-thousandth of the total area. Dad said that it really stood out from the rest and I took this as a compliment.

The new wooden window frames were late arriving, so Dad moved onto the roofless shed. Once he'd completed this building and slotted the windows into place, he felt it was necessary to landscape around the shop to make the entrance inviting. There was ground to prepare, turf and paving to lay, as well as beds to display the plants he would sell. The driveway needed doing so that customers could come and go, and chain-link fencing to be erected at the front boundary.

Due to budgetary restrictions there was no heavy machinery, so Dad had to rely on a wheelbarrow, a spade and a shovel. One evening I noticed that his hands looked strange and on closer inspection I saw that they were completely smooth. There was the odd blister, but not a single fingerprint. I asked how this had happened and he told me that he'd worn them away working on the garden centre.

I've never had criminal tendencies but I remember mentioning that he could now burgle houses and the police would never know it was him because he'd leave no fingerprints behind. I should have known he'd have a sensible reply; he countered with, 'Surely the police would just look for a burglar with no fingerprints.' That one foxed me for years before I realised, after watching an episode of *The Sweeney*, that professional burglars wore gloves, so obviously they don't leave fingerprints either.

The garden centre was coming together. On wet days when Dad couldn't work outside, he erected the shop display units that came free with the products he'd bought and made the others that he needed.

Fortunately Cyril had every woodworking tool an amateur craftsman would ever need or want and helped Dad to fit out the shop. Together they got the inside shipshape in no time.

With the inside all done bar a lick of paint on the walls, Dad turned his attention to the plant display beds and the greenhouse. Once renovated, this glass structure would be used to sell bedding and house plants, as well for propagating his own plants. Growing plants from scratch was a real passion of his, and one that hadn't been satisfied during his landscaping years. When creating gardens for someone else you get as far as planting your design but this is with bought plants, and Dad rarely got to see the gardens he'd worked on after they matured. Needless to say, Cyril was enlisted as assistant craftsman for the renovation of the greenhouse framework and building the outside wooden display beds.

The final task was the signage, a necessity to attract customers. Dad designed a logo that was the outline of a tulip in green inside a yellow circle. He placed this on the left of each of the two large signs he'd ordered, and to the right of each logo it read *The Hamilton Garden Centre* in big letters. I think that hit the nail on the head: people driving past would know that it was a garden centre, and also know that it was owned by a member of the Hamilton family. Not that we'd been there long enough for people to know who the Hamilton family were, although it wouldn't be long before millions knew who Mr Geoff Hamilton was.

I thought that the signs were the final task but they weren't. Apparently no self-respecting business owner could run their business without an efficient security system. Dad couldn't afford to install an alarm so he thought the only option was a guard dog – or at least that's what he told Mum. Funnily enough, he knew exactly where to get just the dog he needed. He visited his parents who were friends with a local farmer whose bitch had just produced a litter of Border collie puppies. There were only two female puppies left so, acting quickly, Dad managed to get his name on one.

When she was old enough to leave her mother, this bundle of fun appeared at home. Dad named her Skip though I don't know why, because she didn't come with a rope and I never saw her skipping. I'm sure he had his reasons. He did well picking her because she turned out to be the less aggressive of the two sisters.

Skip had the annoying habit of biting car tyres as people drove in and out of the garden centre, although this didn't seem to bother Dad. She had a good strong bark, something good in a guard dog, but also used it to let passing cars know that she wasn't happy with them going by. The result was that she spent a lot of her day running up and down the roadside fence chasing and barking at cars. She created such a trench that we thought her legs were getting shorter as her belly gradually got nearer to the ground!

She would occasionally get a bit overexcited when

customers showed interest in her. She would jump up, rest her front legs on the customer's chest and try to lick their face. Most of them were more than happy to pat and stroke her when she did this, although they were more reluctant on wet days when she had muddy paws. Dad was happy to leave her to interact with his customers because he felt she put them in a better frame of mind and therefore more likely to spend – although this was not always the case.

One morning she decided that licking a young boy's face would be a good idea. He'd been patting her head and she felt the need to return his affection. Unfortunately the boy and his dad were just outside the main door into the shop, at the spot where Dad had placed a raised ornamental pond, complete with a small fountain.

While the small boy was heaping attention on Skip, his dad was looking at the fish swimming amongst the aquatic plants on the opposite side of this pond. Skip was loving the attention and she jumped up to rest her paws on the young lad's shoulders. He wasn't ready for this sudden weight and took a step backwards to try and balance himself. That wasn't the best idea bearing in mind his proximity to the pond.

There could be only one result, and that was a rather wet boy. The boy and his dad appeared in the shop, the boy dripping all over the lovely clean floor. Dad was mortified and readied himself for the complaint that was sure to come. There were quite clearly no injuries caused to the boy but the same could not be said about his father, who had come inside the shop to complain to 'the management', about the injuries he'd sustained during this incident: a pulled muscle in his side from laughing so much. Dad even managed to profit from this accident as the man went away with a houseplant, no doubt as a peace offering to his wife for arriving home with a very wet son.

Although she loved the customers' attention, Skip wasn't so enamoured of the people who collected the dustbins and delivered the milk. Often Dad was in the shop serving when the waste collectors arrived on site, so he didn't see what was happening outside – but he could hear the noise. Apparently, Skip would pin the waste collectors by the bins and not allow them to empty them into their lorry.

It wasn't long before Kettering District Council phoned Dad to say that, due to the aggression shown by his dog towards their employees, they would no longer be able to come on site to empty the bins. From then on Dad had to put his bin at the roadside at the end of the drive every Wednesday morning.

This wasn't the last letter he received from a disgruntled supplier; he also had one from the Co-op Dairy, although this one included an added extra – a bill. Dad couldn't understand why he had suddenly got an invoice from the Co-op Dairy head office when the milkman collected the amount due in cash at the end of each week. On closer inspection, he realised that it was a bill for a new pair of wellies. The accompanying letter explained that these were bought to replace the ones Skip had bitten through. We never did find out whether the milkman had done something to upset Skip or whether she had suddenly taken a dislike to him. Anyway, the result was that when Dad put his bins out, he also collected the milk from the roadside verge.

It wasn't long before a fully-grown dog was no longer required as a burglar alarm and she started to come home each evening with Dad. If she was ever left at home, usually at weekends, she needed walking, a task given to whoever was at home and not out playing with friends.

From a very young age I've been interested in growing, having my own little veg plot in the garden and was the only son to take an interest in Dad's occupation, so it was no surprise when I started going straight to the garden centre after school. My homework had to wait until I'd had my horticultural fix.

On one particular occasion, I'd invited a schoolfriend to our house for a meal after school but, as usual, our route took us to the garden centre first. I got stuck into restocking the shelves. After about half an hour, Dad noticed that my friend didn't have the same interest in the garden centre as I did so he suggested that we take Skip for a quick walk and then home. It was late afternoon, Dad was peckish and looking forward to closing up, so that he could head home for something to eat.

My friend and I decided just to walk the dog home so we wouldn't take too long. Unfortunately the journey home took us past the small row of shops on our estate and therefore past Martin's Newsagents. Once Martin's came into view, we were suddenly consumed by the nibbles. My friend fancied a Mars bar and I wanted a packet of salt-and-vinegar crisps, my absolute top crisp flavour. We didn't think about what effect this might have on our appetites for the lovely meal Mum was preparing; everyone knows that when the nibbles hit you, all sense goes out of the window.

Dogs weren't allowed in the shop but there were hooks outside where you could fasten their leads, which is exactly what I did. In we went. I'd been in the shop plenty of times before so knew exactly where the crisp aisle was and quickly collected my two-and-a-half pence bag of crisps before heading for the till. Just as I was paying, I heard an almighty screech of brakes outside.

Suddenly my desire for crisps left me because I felt sick to my stomach. I somehow knew that the screech had something to do with me. Everybody rushed outside, me included, to find a stationary car in the road and a very angry man sitting behind the wheel. There was no obvious reason for him to have stopped so sharply and no evidence of an accident.

I spotted my friend, Mars bar in hand, so I went to untie Skip from her hook. The problem was that the dog hook no longer had a dog attached to it. As I looked around to see where she was, I heard the angry man telling a bystander that a dog had run in front of his car. Although he'd slammed on his brakes, he feared he might have hit it.

It didn't take a genius to work out that the dog had been Skip. My heart sank as the full realisation dawned of the trouble I was in. My friend deserted the sinking ship by deciding that he didn't feel well and needed to go home. Usually I'd have been quite excited at the prospect of one less mouth to feed and more food on the dinner table, but my only concern was how much my stomach was churning.

My first thought was how to retrieve the situation. Perhaps if I could find Skip and, if she was all right, pretend that nothing had happened. No joy there. After a fairly rapid run along all the local streets, I still couldn't see her. That left me with only one option: to go home and face the music. I knew that Dad would be home by now, which meant I would be in BIG trouble when I returned home without his dog.

I walked along St Saviours Road like a man taking the long walk to the gallows without even having the benefit of a last meal before facing the executioner. When our house came into view, I noticed that the drive was empty; Dad must have got waylaid at the garden centre and wasn't home yet. If Skip had made it back home, there was a slim chance that I could escape the hole I was in fairly unscathed.

I ran the rest of the way and burst through the front door, only to be met by three grim faces: Mum, Stephen and Christopher. Blast, they knew! Skip had indeed made it home, just after Dad, but she still had her lead on and there was blood coming out of her mouth. Dad was not taking any chances, so he put her straight in the car and dashed off to the vets. That really wasn't good news because, even at that tender age, I knew that a trip to the vets was expensive. This would be money Dad really couldn't afford to spend. Yes, I was in even BIGGER trouble than I first thought.

It seemed like he was gone for an eternity but actually it was less than an hour before he returned with Skip. The vet had said she was shaken from her ordeal but basically fine. It seems that jerking her head back as the car ran over her lead had probably caused the bleeding.

She might have been fine after this ordeal but I knew that I definitely wouldn't be. Being sent to my room without my meal was to be expected, as was being banned from taking Skip for a walk for the next month. However, a two-week banishment from the garden centre seemed like a life sentence and was far too harsh in my opinion.

I took my punishment on the chin. Dad had taught me a very valuable life lesson about responsibility – and it worked.

Chapter 13

As a boy, teenager and young man, Dad was involved in the Scout movement. He started as a Cub, moving up to being a Scout, before completing his journey as a Queen Scout. Consequently there was never any question that we would all be enrolled into the Cub Scouts as soon as we were old enough.

My own journey started with the 1st Wormley Cub Scout group. I absolutely loved my uniform, just as I loved everything about Cubs – the activities, the badges, camping trips and the friends I made. Dad seemed to know the Scout songbook off by heart and he taught us all the scouting songs he knew, including 'Ging Gang Goolie'! I'm aware that it doesn't rival any of the great pop and rock anthems, but to a Cub Scout it was as anthemic as it got.

Dad had books written by Baden-Powell that he had been bought as a boy. They were very precious to him, and he wasn't giving them up without a fight, which is why we had only borrowed them. We learned a lot about the Cubs – how to behave, what makes a good person, making a fire, knotting, etc. – as well as spotting where

Dad had learned a lot of his parenting techniques.

The 1st Wormley Cub Scout troop was very active and we were always off doing things at weekends. The camping trips were my favourite, even after the trauma of the ill-fated Cornwall camping holiday. When we went on camp, we went to the Scout centre at Gilwell. This was a real adventure for any outdoor, thrill-seeking Cub, a weekend (and sometimes a whole week) miles away from our parents with like-minded enthusiasts. We were left with just a tent and had to rely on our survival skills to stay alive for a whole week – except for Akela, of course, and her many helpers.

While writing this particular section of my book, I looked on a map to see exactly where Gilwell is, something I'd never thought to do before. I knew it was close to home, but would never have thought that we'd only travelled nine miles. I suppose in child distances that's at least five hundred miles, so that's OK.

Whenever I got home from camp it was like the Spanish Inquisition, with thumbscrews thrown in. Dad never collected us from the Scout hut on our return because he was waiting at home, torture equipment in hand, ready to find out what we'd been up to. He was keen to know that we were being properly scouted, as per the Baden-Powell books. Stephen had the same treatment, just in case I'd missed out any vital information. Funnily enough, Dad wasn't concerned about what we'd been getting up to away from home; it was definitely all about the Scouting. And he was never as interested on our return from any of our French summer holidays – *pas besoin de la vis de pouce avec ceux*!

Camping wasn't just restricted to Gilwell. Rather than waterproof the Cornwall tent, Dad would wait until there was the prospect of a clear summer's night before encouraging us to camp in the garden. It was a bit of an odd situation, three young boys sleeping in a tent made for at least six adults. It wasn't hardcore camping, because the tent was almost as palatial as our terraced house.

After several nights of garden camping, Dad was convinced that we were committed to the scouting cause, so he finally got rid of the leaky tent and invested in a two-man tent. This was more like it, this was proper Cub Scout camping *à la Gilwell*. Even better when I invited friends to come round and camp overnight because now we didn't have enough space and were crammed in like sardines – fantastic!

Dad would come out at 8pm and check that all was well and remind us that it was time for us to go to bed. There was obviously no chance of that happening until the early hours; he knew that, we knew that he knew, but he still felt he had to go through the motions.

Dad was keen for all three of us to experience as much as we could to improve us as people. Up to the age of nine I was a very outgoing and confident boy, but all that changed when we moved from Wormley to Kettering. I became shy and was then generally found towards the back of any gathering. I still took part in all the things I'd done before the move – Scouts, playing in school sports teams – and I still made friends, but I was no longer first to do everything.

This was something that didn't go unnoticed. I had just moved up from the Cubs to the local Scout group, so when it was time for our Scout leaders to seek volunteers to represent our group in the local gang show, Dad persuaded me this would be a good thing to do. He felt that it would help to bring me out of my shell. I wasn't pressured into it but, when our Scout leader asked for volunteers to raise their hands, I found my arm rising in the air. It wasn't until I looked around that I realised I was the only one who wasn't overexcited about the possibility of performing in the gang show. What had I done? It could only get worse.

The following week, all the volunteers assembled to allocate each child their part in the show. Obviously I was hoping for a position at the back of the choir. As with all Cub or Scout meetings, we started by singing the national anthem and promising to always do our best. We were then asked several questions before facing the horror of acting out a scene and, even more horrifying, doing a bit of singing. I left the session confident of my spot either at the back of the choir or, better still, as a stagehand.

At the next Scout meeting I discovered my gang show fate: singing! Hadn't they noticed how awful my singing had been during the national anthem? I knew singing in public would not be good for me, but I was also well aware that it would be even worse for the audience. I had put my hand up because Dad had convinced me that they'd only need me to do a bit of acting and, as I'd never been to a gang show before, I accepted what he told me as the truth. He'd heard my singing, so why would he want to subject others to it? It wasn't until we started rehearsals that I realised a gang show was just one song after another with acting squeezed in between.

At the first rehearsal I discovered that not only did I have to stand up in front of a couple of hundred parents, grandparents and anyone else who'd wandered in off the street, but I had to do it dressed as a bridesmaid. I was eleven and very self-conscious so, appearing to think this would make performing easier, the artistic director told me that I wouldn't be alone.

If that was supposed to make me feel better, it didn't – especially when I found out my singing partner was Graham Percival. He was a renowned singer in scouting circles. It could go one of two ways: either my singing would be drowned out by Graham's melodious tones, or I would be heard and my tuneless warbling compared to his beautifully angelic voice. I decided the former was most likely to be the case, which made me feel more confident about my performance, and the rest of the rehearsal evening went without a hitch.

At every rehearsal it was plain to see (and hear) that the rest of the troop were far keener than me to empty their lungs in song. My main objective was to sing as quietly as possible so that nobody could hear me. So why on earth was I chosen to sing one of the solos? What had I done? I hadn't volunteered for that.

I couldn't let Dad down after all the stories he'd told me about his own gang show experiences, so I had no option but to give it my best shot. Like the professional I was, I attended every rehearsal right up until the final week before show night. Not only did I learn both my songs, I even convinced myself that my singing had actually improved. Having said that, I swear that at one rehearsal I saw the artistic director discreetly remove a set of ear plugs after my solo.

A week before the big night, we had a dress rehearsal. After I'd given a rather fine performance, I mentioned the problem I was having with my dress. To start with the colour wasn't right (lilac really didn't suit my rugged, outdoor complexion), but the main problem was that it was far too long. Graham was considerably taller than me and he'd been used as the template for both dresses. This made walking forwards rather hazardous. All these years later, and having had to deal on a daily basis with the combustible combination of the general public and health and safety, I understand what a nightmare this dress was. It was an accident waiting to happen.

We were in full costume for the dress rehearsal and the set was in place. It was then that I discovered that the backdrop for my duet was a church. Apparently the plan was to begin inside the church, open the flimsy door, walk up to the front of the stage and perform. One duet later, involving a solo each in the middle, we would turn, walk back to the church and disappear back through the open door.

The dress rehearsal mostly went according to plan, but in the debriefing later I was told that on the night there would be no hitching up of my dress as I walked. I was very concerned at this revelation.

The evening of the Gang Show's opening performance came and my nerves started to kick in. Eventually I was dressed, literally, and ready to go and embarrass myself in front of my family and lots of other people I didn't know.

Before I knew it I was behind the very rickety church frontage with Graham standing confidently by my side. On our cue, he strode out through the door. I quickly followed, not so confidently. At first I was just trying to walk in a dress with a trail at the back and the front, as well as having to step over the piece of wood on the floor that held the bottom of the church-door frame together. Fortunately this first hurdle went without a hitch but, as I looked up and moved towards the front of the stage, all I could see was row after row of expectant faces. While I'd been waiting for my big entrance, I'd heard the crowd singing along, clapping and cheering. They'd all been having a great time and now they were expecting me to deliver. The level of nervousness shot up.

Without even trying – and probably due to the nerves – I managed to keep my vocal level well below Graham's when the music started. He delivered his solo first, which unsurprisingly he did with confidence and perfectly in tune. Then it was my turn. The spotlight moved over so that it was shining on me. There I was in full view, illuminated so that it looked like I owned the stage.

When I opened my mouth, I was pleasantly surprised with what came out and how tuneful it was. What had just happened? It was a miracle! We completed the rest of the duet and there was rapturous applause. I was overcome by the success of my performance. We bowed, as we'd been instructed to do, and then turned to make our exit.

As we neared the church, I was following Graham when the loud clapping turned to roars of laughter. I'd been overcome by the surge of adulation from the audience and my concentration had lapsed. The inevitable happened, and I stepped on the front of my dress. Suddenly I found myself being propelled forward, arms stretched out in front of me. My hands landed in the centre of Graham's back, shooting him forward too. As he disappeared through the church door, somewhat faster than he'd intended, I hit the floor of the stage with a tremendous thud.

Graham had broken the door but crucially was out of sight; I was lying face down on the stage floor, legs akimbo, in front of everyone. As I rose to my feet, the laughter suddenly became deafening applause. I turned, faced the crowd, bowed, hitched up my dress and scuttled through the now doorless doorway.

Apart from various performers being unable to stand

behind the closed church door while they waited to go on stage, the rest of the performance went swimmingly. And nine months later, I was primed and ready when our Scout leader asked for gang show volunteers. My hands were firmly in my pockets and there they stayed. There was no way on earth that I would put myself through that again, although it has to be said that nobody asked me to!

You may have noticed that at no point during my ramblings about the 1973 Gang Show did I mention Ralph Reader's most famous composition. This is because I seemed to have blanked it from my mind. I'm sure that on the night it was terrific, but after my slight costume mishap I don't remember 'On the Crest of a Wave'.

Cubs was a wonderful experience for me both in Wormley and in Kettering, but moving up to Scouts wasn't so great. Unfortunately, my Scout leader wasn't as easy going and forgiving as our Cub Scout Akela. This was problematic as it doesn't sit well with the genetic and involuntary Hamilton japery.

Due to his workload at the garden centre, Dad took less of an interest in how our weekly Scouts sessions were progressing but Mum received a few notes about discipline. The problem was that the Scout leader wanted to run the troop on military principles, whereas Stephen and I just wanted to have fun. If we'd wanted military principles, we'd have joined the army cadets.

We were in an area we had never been to before, the

area of strict discipline with no deviating from the 'rule book'. Normally Hamilton japery involved no planning or thought, but this man was evoking feelings I'd never experienced before: the desire to plan. I found myself in secret meetings with Stephen, planning ways of bending the boundaries as far as we could without overstepping the line. From a very early age, we'd been aware that there was always a line that we shouldn't cross, though Mr Maguire could testify that it had been overstepped on a few occasions. I understood, more than most, that there were usually drastic consequences to overstepping this line.

Be clear that I was egged on by Stephen. As a consequence, we got quite good at disrupting the disciplinarian Scout meetings, not in a bad way but in a fun way. It became clear that Dad was aware that Mum metaphorically had had her wrists slapped by the Scout leader. Mind you, considering all the pranks Dad got up to when he was younger, he was in no position to discipline us and I'm pretty sure that he secretly admired our efforts.

The straw that finally broke the camel's back was Stephen's but, as before, I gladly went along with it. The theory behind Stephen's idea revolved around our Anglo-French heritage, which surely meant that we only had to sing the British national anthem every other Scout meeting, alternating it with singing 'La Marseillaise' (silently in our heads). Surely this was a noble act of patriotism that honoured both sides of our family?

Every Scout meeting started with the raising of the Union Jack in our scout hall and the singing of the national anthem. Our Scout master noticed the first time we sang 'La Marseillaise' in our heads – that man had the eyes of a hawk. We were taken to one side and told that we had to sing the national anthem and not just stand there in silence. He obviously didn't realise that we were singing – just very quietly. He thought that his telling-off and his power as Scout leader had done the job, because at the next meeting we both sang the national anthem with great gusto. The meeting the following week didn't go so well; it was a silent singing week. He was watching and noticed again, but this time he didn't take the quiet singing quite so well.

We were taken to the other end of the hall and, for the second time in as many weeks, asked why we weren't singing. Although this had been Stephen's idea, he remained silent; maybe he was still silently singing because 'La Marseillaise' is a *long* national anthem. I felt it my duty to fill our Scout leader in on our reasoning and I told it to him straight: as we were half-French, we would only sing the British national anthem at every other meeting.

His face went the brightest red I'd ever seen and he seemed fit to burst. Eventually he exhaled vigorously then asked his assistant to take the remainder of the meeting. Stephen and I were frogmarched home where, in no uncertain terms, he told a very surprised Dad what he thought, and that we were now banned from attending the Scout group.

I hadn't often seen Dad really cross, but this man had obviously touched a nerve. We were standing just behind him when he calmly told our now ex-Scout leader to be more respectful of the traditions and beliefs of others before shutting the door before the man could reply. That was the end of our Scouting experience.

Although Dad was disappointed that our weekly experiences at the Scout hall had come to an end, we came out of the whole experience smelling of roses. Dad was not at all happy with the overreaction of our Scout leader, while Mum was pleased that we were proud to be half-French. I suppose that we shouldn't have been surprised by her reaction but instead have been thankful that she didn't go down the usual route. History tells us that the French have guillotined most of their royal families, so I suppose our Scout leader had a lucky escape.

With the benefit of hindsight, I can't understand how Dad allowed this situation to occur bearing in mind what had happened previously.

Mum was brought up as a Roman Catholic in Paris, a religious upbringing she was keen for her three boys to experience. Dad was happy to go along with it, although he played no part because he wasn't religious in any way. We were named after saints and christened in our local Roman Catholic church. The next step was Sunday school. In Wormley, our local Roman Catholic Church, St Augustine's, was only a couple of miles away in Hoddesdon and we attended Sunday services a few times with Mum, before she signed us up. We were too young to understand that there was something intrinsically wrong, because it was called Sunday school but it was held on a Saturday. Had I realised that this was a sign of the horror that was to follow, I might have resisted being signed up.

Every Saturday morning Mum walked us the two miles to Sunday school, then collected us after the two hours of teaching and indoctrination had ended. We then returned each Sunday morning for the regular service. After a while, we tagged onto another family's tailcoats for the trip to Hoddesdon, while Mum stayed at home and just collected us after the service had ended.

Even though I was not keen on the whole church thing, I was a good boy who did as he was told by his parents. I can therefore state categorically that I was a completely innocent bystander when the biblical eruption occurred.

Being the middle brother, I got on well with both my older and younger brothers, but there was a bit of underlying friction between Stephen and Christopher that spilled out when Dad wasn't present. It was always instigated by Stephen, even though he was old enough to understand the consequences if he started irritating Christopher. He knew that Dad had no time for this type of behaviour and would have defused the situation very rapidly. However, on a Saturday morning Stephen had an ideal opportunity to flex his older brother muscles and teased Christopher whenever he had the chance. Being in Sunday school, there was little opportunity for retaliation.

Without any warning, one Saturday morning we didn't have to get dressed in our smart clothes to go to St Augustine's but were allowed to go out to play instead. What a joyous day that was. I thought that Mum had seen the error of her ways and finally realised that not only was I not enjoying the religious stuff, but that I really needed to be outside on a Saturday morning. Unfortunately my excitement was short-lived, because on Sunday morning we were told to don our best clothes before being marched off to Hoddesdon and Sunday school. In their wisdom, someone had moved it to its proper godly day. What a disaster!

This meant that there was now no break in the bombardment of religion because we went straight from Sunday school into the Sunday church service. I could just about cope with this long stretch, but my two brothers struggled to keep themselves under control. Stephen irritated his younger sibling, and Christopher reacted to that irritation.

Mum was handed a note when she arrived to collect us requesting that she ensured Stephen's and Christopher's behaviour improved as their bickering was upsetting the other attendees. Mum asked Dad to deal with this situation but he was very much of the same opinion as me: we were better playing outside than being in church. Therefore, the parental briefing was somewhat compassionate.

This fateful Sunday saw the culmination of many weeks of irritation and aggravation. It started to bubble up during our Sunday school session but erupted properly during the service. It wasn't so much 'an act of God', more the act of an older brother. We were all sitting in the same pew, in the same order that we sat in the back of the Austin Morris. I was in the middle with Stephen to my left and Christopher on my right. Usually I acted as a sufficient barrier and could keep them apart just by being in the way. On this particular Sunday, it felt like I was preventing the volcanic eruption that was threatening to overwhelm us.

After weeks of being irritated, Christopher finally snapped and lashed out at Stephen. Obviously Stephen couldn't take a passive stance in the face of this act of war and hit back. At this point I did the honourable thing and took a strong stance between the two warring factions. It briefly stemmed the flow, though I think that was due to the space between us on the pews rather than my actions. Unfortunately, Christopher managed to squeeze past me to lash back. Determined to 'do the honourable thing', I decided to assert my self-appointed position of conscientious objector with immediate effect, and quickly moved out of the way.

Full-scale war didn't actually break out, it was more like a pre-war skirmish, but it was certainly too much for the church officials. Stephen and Christopher were sent to opposite ends of the church to sit quietly through the rest of the service. I was left where I was, now happily seated on my peaceful pew.

When we left the church, Mum was not in her usual position on the church steps, but at one side of them talking to the priest. We had a very quiet two-mile walk home with Mum gripping Stephen's hand on one side and Christopher's on the other side.

When we got home, we were sent into the lounge while there was a brief powwow between our parents. Finally Dad appeared at the door. He told Stephen and Christopher that he was very disappointed in their behaviour and sent them to separate bedrooms. There was to be no playing and no reading; they were told to sit and contemplate what they had done.

I watched and listened intently, hoping that I wasn't going to be punished too just because I was there. I wasn't. I did notice that Dad seemed rather relieved to have the going-to-church thing terminated, although probably not in the manner he'd hoped for.

Chapter 14

Although our association with Lord Robert Baden-
Powell ended badly, there are many things I learned at
Cubs and Scouts that still regularly come in useful both
at work and at home. These skills were put to good use at
an early age, because my Christmas present that year was
a practical one: I received my own woodworking set. It
was a wooden box which contained a hand saw, hammer,
screwdriver, set square and special woodworker's pencil.
I was a very practical boy and this was definitely one of
Dad's ideas to encourage me. At eight years old I wasn't
ready to challenge Mr Chippendale, but I was prepared
to make and fix anything. Christmas passed in a flash,
with everything in the house that I perceived in need of
repairing being 'repaired'.

By the time I went back to school, there were bits of
wood in the shed sawn into various lengths. As I had
'fixed' everything in the house, Dad decided to give me
a couple of building projects. However, it wasn't until
March that my own woodworker's brain really kicked
into gear.

My friends had go-karts to race around in, all made

by their dads. I didn't need anyone to make mine because I had all the tools at my disposal. I created the wooden body of what would turn out to be the best go-kart in town out of wood salvaged from Dad's shed. Dad was very encouraging and appeared with a pair of big pram wheels for the back of the cart, complete with axle, and even managed to scavenge a couple of small front wheels for steering. He showed me how to bend the little strips of metal he'd cut to hold the axles to the cart body, then left me to it. I used my Scout knotting skills to tie together several pieces of string as my steering mechanism. I was nearly there; all I needed was to persuade Mum to give me a cushion for the seat and this magnificent construction would be complete.

Even though they didn't show it I could see that both Stephen and Christopher were very impressed with my machine. It was sleek and aerodynamic, and I was positive that it was so good it was capable of breaking the go-kart land speed record.

I thought I'd give it a go. The garden path was surely long enough, so I cleared all large obstacles out of the way. I didn't see the need to sweep the path because the smaller obstacles would not come into play as I literally flew over them. The path was flat, so I needed propulsion. Stephen agreed to push, while Christopher was recruited as the timing mechanism operator. He stood about two-thirds of the way along the path holding Dad's alarm clock. They were keen to help because we all wanted to be immortalised in the *Guinness Book of*

Records for taking part in such an epic record.

I settled myself carefully in the centre of the cushion, took up the strings of my steering mechanism, and pushed my feet firmly against the footrests (blocks of wood). I was ready. I primed my engine (Stephen) with a few encouraging words and we were off. We flew down the path. Then the G-force kicked in and I was hanging onto the strings for dear life.

It wasn't long before I noticed a blur to my left. It was Christopher, so I slammed on the brakes. Braking involved my engine stopping and letting go of the go-kart while I quickly put my feet down on the ground until I came to a slow stop. It was perfectly timed, as I stopped inches from the garden gate.

As all keen record-breakers know, in order to verify the time the test needs to be done twice. I had plenty of time to prepare for this second run as apparently my engine needed to get his breath back. I took this rest time to turn around my speed machine, plump up my driver's seat and remove the dead insects from my hair.

After ten minutes my engine was ready to fire up again. Christopher had moved to the other end of the lawn and signalled that he was ready. On the count of three, we were off. We were just getting up to top speed when disaster struck. First to depart their moorings were the front wheels. The cart nosedived, which then caused the body of the speedster (a plank) to separate from the seat. I followed it.

Once I'd recovered from the initial shock of this near

fatal record attempt, I realised that both my brothers were also on the ground. However, while I was rolling around in pain with gashed knees, they were rolling around clutching their sides in fits of laughter.

Once I'd regained my composure I explained to them and Dad (who had emerged from the house on hearing the commotion) that the G-forces were to blame. It was obvious they had sucked the nails out of the wood, causing the cart to disintegrate in such a spectacular fashion. The letter that I'd already penned to the people at *Guinness World Records* was never signed, sent or ever seen again.

The next go-kart was Dad-made, and it was going to survive use by my children, grandchildren and great-grandchildren. It was impossible for him to make things that didn't last forever.

My next woodworking project was much easier. It was winter and I'd woken in the morning to find a hefty layer of snow lying everywhere. Fantastic – that meant snowball fights and snowman building, although the appeal of the latter had declined as I'd aged. But I had taken to watching *Ski Sunday* and quite fancied the idea of skiing.

From early in my love affair with *Ski Sunday* until I hit fifty, when I finally conceded I was too old, I always wanted to have a go at downhill skiing. Franz Klammer was my favourite skier and I wanted to emulate him. However, unlike Franz, who undoubtedly had natural ability and trained every waking hour of every day, my plan had always been to go to the top of a downhill run, strap on my skis and go for it. Not just go for it, but go for it with no previous training.

There was no way anyone in our family could go skiing in a resort because of the cost, so I decided to do the next best thing. I would make my own and partake in some home skiing. I got out my tool kit, found a couple of old floorboards in Dad's shed and relieved him of them. I measured them carefully and cut them so that they were the same size.

The next job was to attach some string to the middle of them so that I could strap on each ski. All I needed now was a couple of ski poles, and the three-foot bamboo canes that I found were perfect.

I carried my equipment out to the pavement in front of our house and tied the skis to my feet, then I pushed off with my ski poles. Each time, I moved about six inches before the front of my skis became buried in the snow. Unfortunately it hadn't dawned on me that the end of each ski needed to curve upwards to prevent this happening. That job was outside my skill level, so I unfastened my skies, picked them up and carried them back to Dad's shed. I placed them carefully in the same place that I'd found them, and I don't think Dad ever noticed that they'd had another life.

You'd think that this failure would have put an end to my desire to live life on the edge of a ski, but there was no chance of that. Surely there was more to winter sports than just skiing? When you went through the front door of our new house in Kettering, the stairs were directly in front of you. The winter following my tragic – and only – attempt at skiing, I found myself inspired by the Winter Olympics. As usual I was most keen on the downhill skiing, but one day I turned on the television to discover bobsleigh. It wasn't a sport I knew existed but the thought of men flying down an ice track in a metal box excited me. It wasn't long before my urge to get into a bobsleigh and go down an Olympic track overwhelmed me. Sounds familiar? Suddenly, the bobsleigh was right up there with the downhill ski dream.

I continued to be captivated by both the two-man and four-man bobsleigh and studied their techniques, just in case I got the chance. Little did I know that my day was soon to come. Well, almost.

The following summer was wet, as all summers seemed to be during our school holidays, so I was stuck inside with my two brothers more often than I would have liked. My brothers weren't the problem; I was an outdoor child and enjoyed messing about whatever the weather, but Mum put her foot down as she was the one who had to wash my wet, muddy clothes.

On this particular wet day all three of us were at home. Mum had just popped round the corner to the Spar shop to get some sun cream for our upcoming trip to our relatives in France. Over three days of non-stop rain, we'd played every game there was to play and had run out of things to do. Then I noticed that Mum had put out a suitcase upstairs in our bedroom ready to pack our holiday clothes.

Suddenly my mind went into overdrive and I saw the opportunity I'd been waiting for. I dashed downstairs to explain my great idea to Stephen and Christopher – who were not at all keen. I had to work hard to get them onside because all they could see was trouble ahead, not just trouble for me but trouble for all of us if we broke the suitcase. But my plan was bobsleigh-related and so foolproof that it was bound to succeed without any parental knowledge. Eventually I managed to persuade them that all would be well.

The suitcase was one that we'd had for as long as I could remember and was made of what seemed to be incredibly thick cardboard, so thick that it was almost the consistency of wood. My plan was to use it as my bobsleigh down my bobsleigh run. This bobsleigh run had not necessarily been built for this purpose but would be perfect for the job; it would be my Cresta Run. I was sure that this was the way all bobsleighers started in the sport: hurtling down the stairs in a suitcase.

I positioned the suitcase at the top of the stairs and sat in it. The jobs of my two brothers was clear. Stephen was the pusher; he had it easy because he only had to push me two feet before I was over the top step and on my way. Christopher was the Brake Man; his job was to stop me at the bottom of the stairs before I got to the door. At the last minute, I got the collywobbles. I had a vision of Christopher not being able to stop me, and me hurtling through the glass front door. I asked him to open it before he resumed his catching position.

This lapse in proceedings gave Stephen the opportunity to raise the stakes. He'd had an idea: why didn't I curl up in the box before he shut the lid and pushed me off? Apparently this would be more like a real bobsleigh driver's position. The idea appealed. I curled up and he closed the lid. What he didn't mention was that he was going to fasten the clasps so I was locked in.

I felt the suitcase slowly move before tipping forwards, then the speed and the bouncing increased rapidly. I felt the impact as I came off the bottom step and onto the wooden hall floor. I felt one more bump, which I thought was Christopher acting as if he were a train buffer. When I came to a stop, all I could think of was having another go. This was it – this was almost proper bobsleigh.

I seemed to be left in the case longer than I thought practical, even though I was shouting for my brothers to come and get me out so that I could do it again. Then I heard the buttons of the locking mechanism slide together and the clasps ping. Slowly the lid lifted, as did my head. To my horror Mum was looking down at me.

Apparently, as the suitcase shot out of the front door and landed on the edge of the front lawn, Mum was walking along St Saviours Road towards our house and saw what happened. Stephen and Christopher had rushed out of the house to collect me, saw Mum and rushed back in. When asked, they denied all knowledge of my bobsleighing.

The odd thing was that she wasn't cross about my attempt at bobsleigh; she was more worried about the potential damage done to one of our two suitcases. I got out, she checked the case and, once satisfied that all was well, gave it to me to return to our bedroom. The two things that I'm most grateful for from this experience are that I got as close as I'm ever going to get to experiencing the feeling of hurtling down a bobsleigh track, and secondly that I had the foresight not to trust my younger brother's ability to stop a suitcase and got him to open the glass front door. The only thing left to do was to get my toolbox out again and make my own purpose-built bobsleigh, ready for the winter.

It turned out that Dad's early foresight about my woodworking abilities had paid dividends as I moved on from my wooden case of basic tools to taking GCE woodwork at Henry Gotch Secondary in Kettering. I need to start this bit with a true statement: during my time in secondary education, I was far better behaved than Dad was. I can say this confidently because I'd taken note of the stories he'd told me as I was growing up. He was up to tomfoolery on a weekly basis, whereas I restricted mine to probably only once a year. I was a model student who was in the school team for each and every sport, and who ended up as a school prefect in my final year.

When I started secondary school, Henry Gotch was

almost the worst-performing school in Kettering. I'm not seeking to take any credit for its transformation, but when I left it was ranked as the best in Kettering.

I was generally a keen student, but I really loved woodwork. We had an enthusiastic teacher who must have seen that I had previous experience, as well as an enthusiasm for the subject. In my third year we were asked to design and build something for the home. I took to this task with great relish and aimed high; I didn't realise that most students in the class were designing items such as jewellery boxes, tea caddies, bread bins and the like.

My first thought was to build a wall cabinet. I don't know why, because we didn't need one, but I was convinced that when I surprised Mum with a fantastic, wooden wall cabinet she'd be over the moon with joy. I designed the cabinet so that it had open shelving and incorporated a small, locking door for personal things. Even though I say so myself, on paper it looked amazing and I couldn't wait to start constructing it.

This was to be our only project that year, and would be built weekly during our double woodwork lesson. It was left to the teacher to order the correct size and amount of wood for each design. The wood arrived before our next lesson, and I collected my pile and took it to my workstation so that when we arrived for our next lesson we were set to go.

Surprisingly, considering the vagueness of some of the other designs, I was staggered that the teacher had managed to order exactly what everyone needed. He even remembered to add on spare wood to allow for the inevitable sawing mistakes.

My bench seemed to have the whole contents of a woodyard piled next to it; to the amateur woodworkers in the classroom, it must have looked as if I was building a wardrobe. I was a bit concerned myself about the quantity of wood but, saw in hand, I set off on my epic construction project.

During the previous school term we'd learned how to make a dovetail joint, the best joint of them all. It was not an easy task, but I'd virtually mastered it by the end of term. I'd learned how to do the joint and also a very valuable tip: if the joint was a fraction loose, you could fill the gaps with a mix of wood glue and sawdust to make it rock solid and nobody would be any the wiser. This newfound skill had made me determined to construct the outer four walls of my cabinet using dovetail joints to secure the corners. This would ensure that any weight put onto the shelves would not cause a colossal collapse of my masterpiece.

My confidence took an extra boost when my woodwork teacher, the aptly named Mr Birch, agreed to this strategy. I had to cut out slots inside the walls to accommodate the positioning of both the shelves and the dividing walls. If you can imagine a 1970s freestanding, dark-brown MFI lounge wall unit that almost went from floor to ceiling, that's how complicated my wall unit was. Saying that, it was about a tenth the size of its

MFI cousin.

Sliding dividing sections and shelves in and out to make sure they fitted seemed to take up most of my lesson time, but eventually I got to the point where all the slots were in the correct places. The shelves and dividing walls were in and secured. I had put hinges on the small door, so all I needed to do was to pop on the door-locking mechanism and apply a coat of varnish to the whole thing. The lock wasn't provided by the school, so I went to our local hardware store; the one I wanted wasn't in stock, so it had to be ordered.

The end of our year was fast approaching and the lock took longer than expected to arrive at the hardware store so, under the guidance of my teacher, I decided to mark out the position of the lock and drill the keyhole then varnish the whole cabinet. Once varnished, it looked spectacular and I knew that Dad would think it definitely worthy of an accolade – although I must admit to only ever having heard him attribute this accolade to his own efforts. However, I was sure my masterpiece would be 'a monument to a master craftsman'. It had that accolade written all over it.

Our final woodwork lesson was on the last Thursday afternoon of the academic year. I'd popped into the hardware store every Saturday for four weeks, a two-mile diversion to my journey home, in the desperate hope that my lock would be there. Finally, on the Saturday before the last lesson, it was waiting with its four screws in a little brown paper bag. Once I crossed the hardware shop owner's hand with 25p, I went home longing for Thursday to come round, unlike the rest of the children in my year, who were all focused on Friday, the last day of term.

Thursday finally arrived. As I did most days, I met up with a couple of friends on my way to school. One told me with great excitement in his voice that his dad had said there'd been a fire at our school during the night. Like any fourteen-year-old boy, I enjoyed the sight of a bright-red fire engine. Maybe the firemen were still putting out the fire.

On our mile-long walk to school we passed several other children who all had a variation on the story, but the recurring rumour was that six fire engines had attended. This rumour escalated our levels of anticipation and excitement. We knew it wasn't just a fire in a waste bin, although we couldn't imagine where the fire could have been. Obviously the science block seemed to be the most logical place.

We arrived at school just in time to avoid being the first on the list of late pupils and getting a detention, so I had to dash straight to class for registration. As was the case every day, this was followed by assembly. As usual the headmaster rose to open proceedings, but this morning they were somewhat different. He wasn't the smiliest of people, but I suppose he'd been in education a long time.

He stood up with a very sombre look on his face and gravely announced that there had been a fire at the school during the night. We already knew that, but I needed to know more. He continued by telling us all that we weren't going to be able to use the top playground that day or the next, the last two days of term.

More than forty years later, I still tremble when I recall what followed. The headmaster said that any pupils who had art, metalwork or woodwork would have these lessons replaced by a tutorial. I was panic-stricken and clutched onto the small brown paper bag in my trouser pocket. The head hadn't finished. He continued that the art and craft building was strictly out of bounds. He put great emphasis on the 'strictly' bit so we knew that if we went anywhere near it there would be big trouble – and probably a trip to see the teacher who had the cane in his desk drawer.

The metalwork building contained gas bottles so presumably that was the source of the fire and the whole block had been cordoned off because of problems in that building. The long and the short of it was that I would now have to wait until after the summer holidays before I could finish off my masterpiece. I'd told Mum that I was making her birthday present in woodwork, so it would be a bit late as her birthday was in the middle of June. It also meant that I'd have to spend hard cash and buy her a temporary present.

Being a good boy who always did as he was told, I followed my headmaster's instruction almost to the letter until my friend told me he'd heard that a group of pupils were going to take a crafty look at the fire-damaged building from the closest possible point without infringing the headmaster's cordon. My friend and I followed the fifth formers, who seemed to know where the fire had been and the best point to view it. We sneaked round part of the playing field like a group of paratroopers on a mission; our route should render us invisible to the teachers keeping a lookout from the staff room window.

While crouching and moving slowly along the bank at the edge of the school playing field, I heard the rumour coming down the line that the fire had been started by a disgruntled fifth former who'd been expelled for swearing at the metalwork teacher and threatening him with physical violence. Phew, my assumption was correct: he'd have targeted the metalwork block.

As we came around the back of our languages block, the art and craft building came into view. A fifth former told me to keep my head down because that meant that if a member of staff spotted you, they'd only see the top of your head and couldn't identify you. As I crept forward the building came into full view and the full horror became apparent.

I couldn't believe what my eyes were telling me. The idiot who'd had a problem with the metalwork teacher had only gone and set fire to the woodwork building! I wondered if I'd passed my eleven-plus and made it to Kettering Grammar School, would the pupils there have had more sense and managed to set fire to the right building?

The art and craft building was prefabricated and obviously full of wood, so it had gone up like a petrol-soaked rag. The individual prefabricated buildings were joined together to create a block so we could access other classrooms without having to go outside, so it was amazing that the fire brigade had managed to stop the fire spreading to the art and metalwork classrooms. It was obvious that the woodwork classroom couldn't be saved because where it once stood was a pile of burnt and charred wood and wet ash.

At this point, I pulled my small brown paper bag from my trouser pocket. I opened it, extracted the shiny brass lock and gazed at it for a few minutes. All I had left of my 'monument to a master craftsman' was my purchased lock. My beautifully crafted cabinet had gone up in smoke.

I never found out who the fire-starter was, but I hung onto that lock for the next twenty-seven years before I managed to persuade myself that it was time to let go. I've not found it possible to forgive the arsonist, though.

In conciliatory mode, Dad said that I should build another cabinet at home. He even offered to buy the wood, but I was too devastated to accept – even though it would have worked out to be cheaper than the original because I'd already spent 25p on the lock.

Dad was very impressed with the brass lock and took the time to examine it properly. He had a love of old-fashioned hardware stores primarily because, as was the case with the one we had locally, they were family-run and stocked everything he needed. Whenever he came across one, he couldn't pass by without popping in to see what they had. Whether he really needed it or not, he always felt obliged to emerge with something in a small brown paper bag, on the basis that 'you never know when you might need one'.

On a trip to research a *Gardeners' World* programme, he popped into a little hardware store in a town not too far from home. He was so excited by this little gem and told me that it was like an Aladdin's cave with everything you could ever want or need. The added bonus for Dad was that Mr Abbott, the owner of this hardware store was dour and, in Dad's opinion, had no sense of humour. To be fair, he probably didn't have the same terrible sense of humour as Dad and therefore didn't find Dad's quips particularly funny. This was the point that the Hamilton Curse kicked in and Dad began his mission.

He told me that he would keep going into this store until he managed to generate some sort of humorous reaction from the owner. He was hoping for full laughter but a chuckle would do. Each time he went in, Dad already had a funny line in his head. After browsing for a while, he'd strike up a conversation and wangle it so that he could deliver his line. It never raised even a flicker at the corner of Mr Abbott's mouth. This went on for about three years. When Dad set his mind on something, he stuck to it and this became the shop he visited most, but with no success. In the end he had to admit that this current plan wasn't going to work, although he wouldn't give up and formulated a different approach.

He decided that, instead of amusing the shop owner, he would be satisfied with amusing himself while hoping against hope for a reaction. It wasn't difficult for Dad to decide what he would say; he could always think of the worst thing to come out with at the best time. He decided to ease into it gently, just in case he got caught out the very first time.

Once he was ready, he went through the usual ritual of striking up a conversation. When the time was right, he asked, 'Mr Abbott, I need a round handle. Do you stock a range of wooden knobs?' He got the reply he was expecting and was directed to the place he passed on every visit where these knobs were plainly on display.

During the next two visits Dad varied his question, each time getting closer and closer to his killer question. On one visit he asked, 'Mr Abbott, do you have a cabinet knob?'; on the next, 'Do you have a smaller knob than this one?' as he thrust a small wooden knob in front of him.

The question changed slightly until one day he felt he'd reached the point he was aiming for. He walked into his favourite shop and was immediately greeted by the owner. Dad was ready and said, 'Hello, Mr Abbott, have you got a small knob?' He was barely able to contain his amusement and delight.

Then came the anticipated, straight-faced reply: 'Yes, Mr Hamilton, they're just over there, next to the large ones.'

This to and fro continued for several years, although Dad never did get even the slightest smirk. Whenever I accompanied him, I always hung back, not wanting to be party to his jape in case Mr Abbott was indeed aware of what Dad was doing. I was pleased when the shop owner retired and the shop was sold, because I was very uncomfortable when visiting the shop and facing this poor man after so many 'small knob' questions. The one good thing to come out of this is that if I live to be one hundred and fifty, I will never need to buy a small wooden knob. There are boxes full of them!

If any viewer of *Gardeners' World* ever wondered why everything needed a knob, now you have your answer. This was taking the Hamilton desire to try and raise a smile in any situation into a lifelong mission. Unfortunately Dad never achieved his goal, although he must be resting very peacefully knowing that there will always be a small knob somewhere in the gardens at Barnsdale.

This ability to say exactly the right thing at the right time for maximum effect was a talent passed down the male side of his family. This was only too evident at Rosa's funeral. As a family, we were not particularly good at funerals. It wasn't that we couldn't control ourselves emotionally, it was more of the case that something always seemed to go wrong.

The first occasion in Dad's memory was obviously Great-grandma Ali diving into Alf's grave when he was buried. Then there was Cyril's funeral in their home town of Uppingham. We three boys were standing in age order. During the first hymn I realised that too many people could hear my terrible singing, so I decided to mime.

About two-thirds of the way through the service, I turned to Stephen and whispered that I was bursting for the toilet. He said that he was too. Christopher heard this exchange and chipped in with the same comment. As the funeral ended and Cyril was being carried out to the hearse to be driven down to the graveyard about a hundred yards down the hill, I leant across to Dad and asked where the nearest toilet was. Fortunately for all our bladders, there was one in the marketplace about fifteen yards from the church door. Dad told us to be quick.

We waited respectfully for the hearse to pull away and the mourners to start following the cortège before dashing off in the direction of the public toilets. Knowing the importance of speed, none of us loitered, but when your bladder is at capacity it can take a while. When we emerged from the public lavs, there was no sign of the hearse. Moving towards the edge of the market place, we saw that the hearse and mourners had arrived at the graveyard. We were further behind than expected, so the only thing to do was run.

We ran like the wind. I didn't look to see where my

brothers were as my eyes were firmly fixed on what was happening at the bottom of the hill. The distance between the top and bottom of the hill had never seemed that far when we travelled it in the car.

We made it just in time and joined the other family mourners, but we were definitely the only ones panting heavily at the graveside. To be honest, I couldn't really hear what the vicar was saying over the sound of my heavy breathing, but it wasn't long before Cyril had been popped into the beautifully prepared hole and we were heading off for the wake.

The trip back to Dad's car in the marketplace was more sedate than the manic dash down the hill a few minutes earlier. The wake was being held at Rosa and Cyril's bungalow and, as we expected, Rosa had provided a magnificent spread. I think virtually everyone who attended the church service and burial also came to the wake. There were a lot of people crammed into the lounge, many whom I'd never seen before. It wasn't surprising because Rosa's buffet provision was legendary.

The three of us decided to congregate in our own little group in order to avoid having to talk to old people. I'd never been to a wake before so I wasn't sure of the protocol. At nineteen, I was aware that the death of a close family relative was a sad affair but Cyril had been a very funny man who would have hated people being miserable at his wake.

It seemed that he even made sure his final act was funny. He'd been recovering at home from his fifth moderate heart attack when he felt the need to use the facilities. Not long after this, Rosa heard a terrific bang coming from the bathroom. She dashed in to find Cyril lying on the floor next to the toilet, trousers round his ankles. She cradled him in her arms for a short while before he passed away.

It was like he'd written the script. He would have been well aware, as were we, that there was no way that Rosa would tell anyone that Cyril had died on the toilet. She would go as far as to say it happened in the bathroom but no further.

When I heard laughter coming from behind me, it was no surprise. I'd been reminiscing with my brothers about the funny things Cyril had done in our lifetime and we'd also been giggling. However, this laughter from behind us went on a bit too long so I turned to see what was happening. Well, I could have died – not a good thing to do at a wake.

The shock of what I saw was seismic. I looked again carefully, to make sure I was certain what I'd just seen, then turned back to tell my brothers. They were somewhat confused when I said, as quietly as possible, that Cyril was sitting in his chair. Initially they both thought that I'd been on the alcohol but when they looked they had to agree. It was definitely Cyril. How an earth could he be sitting in his chair when we'd just witnessed him being buried? Was this Cyril's greatest prank? Had he faked his death and then turned up at his own wake?

There were only two ways to find out the truth: the first was to go and ask Cyril what had happened, and the second to ask Dad. Bravely, I took the second option.

Dad regularly told me that I had a lucky streak, and this was a perfect example. It turned out that it wasn't Cyril but Maurice, Cyril's best friend. At first I found it very odd that someone would have a best friend who was their doppelgänger, but when I thought about it I realised it was the perfect scenario for someone like Cyril – but it still didn't remove the strangeness or stop me being surprised by the weird feeling of seeing Cyril at his own wake!

Cyril's funeral was eight years after Mum and Dad were divorced. As my brothers and I couldn't drive, Dad picked us up from Kettering on the day of the funeral. Over those eight years, I could probably have counted on one hand the number of civil words that were spoken between my parents, so it wasn't surprising to me that the drive to Uppingham was somewhat quiet.

We sat in the back and Mum was in the front passenger seat. Dad asked three simple, polite questions and got one-word replies to all of them. During the funeral they stood at each end of their line of children. However, not long after arriving at Rosa's for the reception, Dad emerged from the kitchen, found Mum sitting on the settee and asked if she'd like a drink. Usually the only alcoholic drink she consumed was a glass of wine at Christmas, otherwise it was soft drinks all the way – very strange for a woman who came from France, the home of red wine. Sure enough she went for a blackcurrant and lemonade, but Dad told her that on a day like today she should have something slightly stronger. She thought for a while and, after asking how tall the glass was, opted for an inch of Dubonnet with six inches of lemonade. Now Dad always gave the impression that his maths was good, but unbeknown to Mum the drink returned with a 3:4 ratio of Dubonnet to lemonade.

During the reception we didn't really notice anything, but what a contrast on the journey home! Mum wouldn't stop talking; it was like she was in the company of an old friend she hadn't seen for years. This was the only time I ever saw my mum inebriated, but not the only time I saw Dad's very crafty side.

Just a year after Cyril, it was Great-grandma Ali's turn to pop off, some fifty years after Alf was buried. Ali had been in what we used to call an old people's home for the previous five years. This was not the way Ali wanted to spend any of her time, let alone her final years and we somehow knew that there would be a payback, one final act of defiance.

When the end came it was expected; she had deteriorated during her last year, having finally succumbed to dementia. She passed away on the ninth of December 1981, aged ninety-three.

Rosa took on the responsibility of organising the funeral on her own this time, having had help from Dad and Tony for Cyril's funeral. This she did by using her legendary skills of moderately pressuring people, always with a smile, to get what she wanted.

The date was set for the church service and burial, the buffet menu written, the ingredients put on a shopping list, and the bungalow was in the process of being cleaned from end to end ready for the reception. The cogs were turning with military precision. All was set.

꽃

Ali's route to the old people's home was unusual. While at home one afternoon, she tripped on the edge of the rug in her lounge, fell forward and knocked herself out when her head hit the coffee table on her way down. It was an afternoon in January and she was on the floor all night.

As she was living in Ashley at the time, Cyril used to pop over most mornings to see if she was all right and if she needed anything. He had a key and, when there was no answer to his knock, he let himself in. He found Ali awake but still on the floor so, after quickly checking her condition, he called her GP who advised calling an ambulance.

Ali ended up in St Mary's Hospital, Kettering where she was treated for hypothermia. The doctor in charge tried to persuade her that she was at an age where she needed live-in care, and the best solution would be if she moved in with Rosa and Cyril. The thought of this had a more devastating effect on her than the hypothermia. She wouldn't even think about such a move. She was adamant that she was going home and that was that.

She went home and lived a perfectly normal life for the next twelve months or so, until she decided that her bedroom needed rearranging. It was a job she'd been meaning to get round to for a long time and she now felt it just had to be done and today was the day. She had invited a friend round for tea and biscuits that afternoon and after the friend had departed Ali didn't have time to empty the chest of drawers and wardrobe, move them to their new position and refill them. She came to the obvious conclusion: they would have to be moved as they were. These were substantial items of furniture she and Alfred had been given as wedding presents. She was only eighty-nine years old at the time and believed she was more than capable of shuffling around furniture, full or not. Unfortunately this family trait of just getting on and doing whatever needed doing had also been passed on to both Dad and me.

Before starting to move the chest, she had the foresight to remove the drawers and that move went according to plan, replacing the drawers once *in situ*. She knew she could move the wardrobe while it was still full. This went according to plan, and the room was now just as she wanted it – perfect.

Later, when preparing her dinner, she started to feel uncomfortable. She had a bit of a twinge in her groin but thought nothing of it – at her age she was used to aches and pains – but over the next couple of days this twinge gradually became a pain. It was then that she made her fatal mistake: she phoned the doctor.

The doctor decided that it was important enough for a home visit and, after examining her, his diagnosis was a groin hernia that needed surgery. She was sent to Kettering General Hospital for this minor procedure. It should only have been a short stay but this was her second hospital visit due to home incidents in twelve months, and the doctor deemed her no longer able to look after herself.

After meeting and discussing the situation with Rosa, Ali's fate was sealed: either she moved in with her daughter and Cyril, or she had to go into a care home. Rosa signed the papers condemning her to life in a home. Dad pointed out at the time that nobody had asked Ali if she felt it was in her best interests, but his remarks fell on deaf ears.

I was a teenager when Great-grandma Ali went into the home, and I didn't visit as often as I should. She'd always been there and I assumed that there was no rush because she'd be there for a good while yet. Even Dad only visited her a few times; he told me that it was gut-wrenching for him to see his beloved grandma in a place where she was so unhappy, sitting in a chair all day with little or nothing to stimulate her. He knew that she was better dead than going through that daily mental torture. Ali wasn't your typical ninety-year-old, she had the mental and physical capabilities of someone twenty years younger. She shouldn't have been put in there.

Two days before Ali's final farewell, the funeral

director rang Rosa with the news that the ground was so frozen they couldn't dig the necessary hole for the coffin to be popped into. According to the forecast, the weather wouldn't improve significantly for two weeks so they would have to cancel the funeral and reschedule it. I'd heard of sports events being cancelled due to frozen ground, but never a funeral.

Rosa's precisely planned event was thrown into disarray and she was gutted. It was almost as if Ali was having the last word in her battle of wills with her daughter; it was her last hoorah, and Rosa's penance for putting her mother into a place that she hated. After many phone calls, the funeral went off without a hitch albeit two weeks late.

Some years later, when Rosa succumbed to stomach cancer, yet again the funeral didn't quite pan out as it should. The responsibility for that has to be laid squarely at Dad's door. To be fair, even after years of Rosa being Rosa, she had an excellent turnout of friends for the church service. However, one notable person was missing: the local vicar. Rosa had been a regular churchgoer and, as she would tell you, a pillar of the community – but she did like things to be right. It seems that he was on holiday, so the service was taken by a stand-in vicar. All went without incident.

The service was held in the same church in Uppingham that was the venue for both Cyril's and Ali's funerals. I was ready this time and made sure that I visited the gents' toilet before I went in; unlike Cyril, Rosa would not have found one of her grandchildren running after the hearse to catch it up particularly humorous.

We all walked behind the hearse and down the same hill to the same graveyard. We knew that they had bought a double plot and had thought this would place them side by side. Nobody on our side of the family was aware that you could go one on top of the other and we hadn't noticed that Cyril had been lowered into a very deep hole at his funeral. It was only at the graveside that we discovered they'd just bought the one plot.

I stood on one side of Dad, while Stephen and Christopher were at the other, as close to the hole as we could. Fortunately this time nobody dived into it. Walking from the church to the graveside, Dad hadn't said a word to anyone; he must have been focusing on what he needed to say.

The comment ranks in the top three of Dad's finest and was made at the perfect moment; it would have made Cyril laugh, a lot. As the coffin started its downward journey and disappeared beyond the edge of the grave, Dad delivered one sentence with impeccable timing: 'Poor old bugger. She was on top in life, now she's on top in death.'

I nearly bit through my lip in my desperation not to burst out laughing. The people behind us must have wondered why the shoulders of the four of us were jigging up and down. The result was tears, but not from sadness. There was no sadness because in the end Rosa had been in so much pain that her death was a blessed relief. These were tears of pain from the massive effort we were making not to laugh out loud.

Chapter 15

Recognition and popularity on television were something that Dad took in his stride, and he attributed his ease in front of the camera to the genes passed down by his Grandpa Alf. He was well aware that being stopped in the street, in a shop and even while having a meal in a restaurant, were all part of the job. He told me that without his viewers he wouldn't have a television career and a very big part of that was the off-screen stuff.

He was more than happy to be stopped by people who wanted to talk to him, because it was always about his favourite subject, gardening. He was far less comfortable when the desire to talk was driven by the fact that he was on television, and more precisely BBC 2's *Gardeners' World*. He was often embarrassed by the supposed status fame brought. At the end of the day he was just a normal bloke who had found his forte, the thing he was born to do.

He certainly wasn't a seeker of fame. He didn't want to attend celebrity parties, open shopping centres or turn on Christmas lights. All he wanted to do was to get as many people as possible to feel what he did when he was in the garden, to experience the emotions he experienced when he propagated a plant. He wanted them to understand how horticulture improves mental health, and to improve their general health too by getting them to 'grow their own'. He wanted to encourage them to garden organically and to promote the ecosystems that are so important to the survival of our planet. Most of all, he wanted everyone to understand horticulture and how it could improve their lives.

He did this in the only way he knew, by being himself. There was no act, no false persona; what you got on the television was what you got in real life. I'm absolutely certain that this was the reason people took to him so readily, loved him, took up gardening because of him or improved their gardening because of his instruction on *Gardeners' World*.

He'd started his rise to television stardom by presenting an Anglia Television production called *Gardening Diary* in 1971. As was to be expected from a Hamilton, it wasn't the usual route taken into television presenting. He didn't apply for the position as presenter but was put forward by a horticultural industry friend of his, something Dad was unaware of at the time. This friend had applied for the presenter's job on a new programme, but after auditioning he was told he was not what they were looking for. Unselfishly, and unknowingly, he was about to propel an unknown onto his road to immortality.

He asked the Anglia Television representatives what

sort of presenter they were seeking. After they explained, he decided to help them in their search and told them that the man they needed was someone he knew, Geoff Hamilton. He picked up one of their pens, scribbled Dad's phone number on a piece of paper and left the room. At the time, he was the only person there who knew he was right.

The next day, a secretary from Anglia Television phoned Dad and asked him if he was interested in coming for an audition to present a new gardening programme they were developing. After recovering from the shock of this unexpected phone call he was given a brief explanation of the job. He said that he'd like to attend very much and was given a day and time.

On the day, he set off for Norwich feeling both nervous and excited at the prospect of a new experience. He had no real idea of what to expect, which is where the nerves stemmed from, but the excitement came from his brain working overtime during his long drive. Dad particularly loved teaching the uninformed about everything horticultural. He knew from talking to customers at the Hamilton Garden Centre and giving out lots of free advice that this was an opportunity to do the same thing to many more people.

It was fairly obvious that his destiny was to be an educator. All he was taking to the audition was himself; he'd been self-employed all his working life, apart from his very short stint working for Cyril, so he had no references. He'd decided that he'd just turn up and wing it.

He'd been fairly confident of success because he believed that he was the only one they were seeing, but when he got to the studios he found he was one of six. By the time he arrived, they had already seen two of the candidates and they were running very late. Dad's confidence started to ebb. The delay could only mean that the two previous candidates were so good that their auditions had continued longer than anticipated.

The next candidate went in. He was the one directly before Dad, and he emerged a full hour later, by which time Dad had very little of his fingernails left. He expected to go straight in but they kept him waiting for a further ten minutes, presumably to discuss the merits of the chap who'd just been in. Finally, Dad was called and went in. This was his big moment, his time to shine and the start of a new career. Fifteen minutes later, he was back out and on his way home.

Even before he got to his car, he had persuaded himself that his chances of landing the presenter's job were nil. How could he even be in the running when he'd only spent a quarter of the time auditioning compared to the others? To make matters worse, not only had he travelled more than two hours to get there (meaning he had another two-hour trip back home) but he'd also paid someone to man the garden centre for the day. What a waste of a day!

By the time he got home, he really was down in the dumps. He hadn't said anything to us children prior to the audition, but he spilled the beans that evening.

I asked if he could be mistaken, but he was clear: it was the end of his budding television career. It was the only explanation for being despatched so quickly. He said that he didn't get even a chance to make them understand what he could offer. All the ideas he had. Then he told us that it didn't matter, it was just another of life's many experiences.

Within the week he received a letter with the Anglia Television logo stamped on the front. He wasn't surprised to get a response so quickly after such an awful audition; it was obviously his rejection letter. He left it on the table and didn't open it until the following morning, just before he set off to open up the garden centre.

To his utter amazement, it wasn't a rejection but a letter offering him the position as presenter of *Gardening Diary*. If he hadn't been sitting down, he'd have fallen over. Dad was never lost for words but on that morning, when I asked him what it said, he opened his mouth and nothing came out.

During his first meeting with his new producer, one of the Anglia Television representatives who'd been present at the audition, Dad asked him how he'd managed to get the job after such a short interview. The producer replied that they knew he was the perfect man for the job within the first five minutes but thought they needed to show some sort of professionalism by extending the interview to fifteen minutes. Apparently nobody else was even considered after they'd spoken to him.

This new gardening show had been devised to be the partner programme to the already well-established *Farming Diary*. It used a similar format, something television programme makers have been doing for years; once they find a format that works, they'd repeat it endlessly. However, the difference being that *Gardening Diary* was to be studio-based, unlike the outdoor *Farming Diary*.

This was a real shock to Dad because many of his ideas were not workable in that sort of format. He needed an outside space and there wasn't one. But he made plans anyway; he would go along with their format, develop ideas that could be demonstrated inside and not rock the boat, while focusing on the greater plan. He was sure that the first series would be successful, and that would give him the leverage he required to get some outside space.

Ideas for this series flowed. To be honest, it was like a tsunami of ideas, many of which were only really suitable for the second series. Dad had these typed out and put them in a folder, ready for the end-of-series review and next-series planning meetings.

The first programme was recorded and broadcast on a Sunday morning in order to catch gardeners before they started their Sunday gardening ritual. During the first recording, Dad set out his stall with his regular opening line: 'Hello, good morning and welcome'. I thought that was a perfect start, but then I'd never watched David Frost so I didn't realise until some years later that

Dad has stolen his perfect televisual greeting!

As they were recorded and broadcast, the programmes went from strength to strength and gained more viewers each week. It was clear that Anglia Television had been right to select him; the viewing figures were well beyond anything the company had expected or hoped for.

The producer was already talking about how they could expand their offering for the next series. This was like music to Dad's ears. The end-of-series meeting was looming so, with the producer in such a positive frame of mind, Dad took his opportunity to remove his ideas from the folder. Unfortunately, the meeting didn't go as well as he had hoped. When Dad started to talk through his ideas for the next series, his producer's face didn't light up. Previously he had been positively excited; this time he was positively unexcited. Not even a detailed description of Dad's ideas could raise any enthusiasm.

Nothing could have prepared Dad for what he was about to be told. The producer announced that Anglia was not commissioning another series. The news was like a dagger to Dad's heart. The producer explained that there had been a budget meeting and the accountants had told the board that they needed to save some money. The accountants had identified that the two programmes that brought in the least advertising revenue around their time slots were *Gardening Diary* and *Farming Diary* – and one of them had to go.

The board took their comments on board. As the company was based in an agricultural region, they decided that they couldn't cancel *Farming Diary* so *Gardening Diary* had to go. To Dad, it seemed like the accountants were in charge and had the real power. The saddest thing was that it wasn't about the popularity of the programme, or the interest generated by it, but all about the advertisers. Dad was cast aside. Although he left Anglia with his producer's praise and gratitude for his professionalism still ringing in his ears.

In all the years I knew him, one of Dad's great traits was that he was such a positive and forward-looking bloke, so it's hard for me to reconcile now why he felt that this minor setback was the end of a great television career. He thought he'd been cut short in his prime – just goes to show what he knew! It also goes to show why you should never listen to a parent in negative mode.

This short-but-sweet flirtation with the world of television was something Dad had genuinely enjoyed, but he was now back in the 'real world' and had to turn his full focus on the garden centre. When I say his full focus, I actually mean most of it! He'd been bitten by the media bug and realised that he was actually quite good at it. Consequently he decided not to let his ideas for *Gardening Diary* go to waste but to use them as a basis for a couple of articles in gardening magazines. He saw potential in the media but this time wanted to try the written word.

Sitting in his office in front of his new typewriter on a quiet Monday morning at the garden centre, he began to type. A couple of hours and several sheets of paper later (no Tipp-Ex in those days) and he was done. There was definitely a good chunk of Rosa within Dad, because he never thought to start small; small was definitely not Rosa's style.

The obvious starting point would have been the *Kettering Evening Telegraph*, a local paper that would offer him the opportunity to perfect his writing skills. Instead he went straight to the top and sent off his two articles to the top gardening national newspaper at the time, *Garden News*.

Well, why not? The publisher was a fairly regular customer at the Hamilton Garden Centre, and some time earlier he'd asked Dad if he'd ever thought of writing because he had such a good way of putting things across. All he had to do was to convert verbal instructions into written words. Dad was far too busy with the garden centre and family life to contemplate writing, so this generous piece of advice had gone to the back of his mind. Until now.

Before sending them off, Dad read and reread his articles several times. He was sure that they were up to the standard required. Being a regular reader of *Garden News*, he couldn't see any reason why they shouldn't be published – which is why he was somewhat bemused when the paper didn't immediately reply. It had only been a couple of weeks, but Dad was keen to get this new side of his career up and running. Surely they'd want to snap him up before someone else got wind of this new literary talent?

Every day he met the postman at the garden centre gate, not just because he needed to due to the dog–postman conflict but because he felt that it might speed up the reply. With every passing day, and with no letter arriving, Dad became more and more resigned to the fact that they had not seen any potential in the articles he sent them.

He decided not to dwell on yet another media setback, but instead to progress another idea he had, which was to create a yearly diary of jobs to do in the garden. This was something that he would write and sell exclusively in the garden centre. It would be different to anything else on the market in that it wasn't going to be in book form. Instead he would section out the jobs to be done throughout each month, write them on cards, which would be kept in a file-like box under monthly headings. The unique selling point of this scheme was the ease of access to individual jobs, and that you only needed to take one card into your garden rather than a whole book. This idea wasn't a dead cert to make him his millions, but he believed it was a sure-fire winner all the same.

Having given up all hope of a positive outcome from *Garden News*, Dad set about his new diary project with gusto and filled every spare moment with writing. Little did he know that the *Garden News'* best-known writer, Geoff Amos, had been handed the envelope containing his two articles. In the 1970s this was not the usual way people got to write for gardening publications; usually the publication approached well-known gardeners and asked them to contribute. They certainly weren't used to some relatively unknown upstart horticulturalist audaciously assuming they could wheedle their way in by sending unsolicited articles! Unsurprisingly, Geoff Amos put the envelope on his desk for a couple of days because he thought it was a contribution from a reader hoping to get onto the letters' page. He was blissfully unaware that it was a contribution from a reader trying to take his job.

It was a very busy time in the gardening calendar, so also a very busy time for everyone at *Garden News*. Dad's envelope sat on Geoff's desk for a couple of days, then a couple of weeks and then a couple of months. Eventually Geoff rediscovered it and decided he ought to repay the effort taken by the reader of their newspaper and see if their letter was worthy of publishing.

He started to read and quickly realised that it wasn't a letter after all. He was captivated. As soon as he finished the final sentence, he was straight out of his seat. After knocking on the *Garden News* editor's door and being asked to enter, he burst through proclaiming that the editor must read the article too.

Back in sunny Kettering, unaware of the commotion he had caused in the *Garden News* offices, Dad had finished January's jobs for his new box calendar and was just starting on February's tasks. He decided to take a break because he was suffering from a mental block and couldn't get his thoughts organised. February is not an easy month in the garden, so maybe this struggle was to be expected. He felt some air might help and walked down to the garden centre gateway, where he'd erected a home-made letterbox specially for his dog-fearing postman. Sure enough there were letters in it. Tucking a bundle of envelopes under his arm, he set off for the nursery beds to check on the watering situation.

To keep his plants in tip-top condition, they needed to be watered – more so on windy or warm days. Dad carried out this essential task regularly to make sure no plants were missed. This time it was fruitless as every plant pot seemed wet enough, although seeing the potted roses gave him a starting point for his list of February jobs: pruning shrub roses. He wondered why he'd not thought of it before as it was a job he'd done every February since leaving college.

Back in the office, he put the bundle of mail top of his filing cabinet before settling down in front of his typewriter. He wanted to strike while the thoughts were fresh in his mind. The dos and don'ts of rose pruning flowed from his fingertips and he battered the typewriter keys with a rhythmical precision as he forged on.

He worked without interruption until well past lunchtime when his growling stomach finally got the better of him. He made a cup of tea and grabbed his sandwich box from the potting shed; as it was the coldest place in the garden centre, it also doubled as the fridge. Sandwich in hand, he settled back in his chair and continued to work. The rate at which he typed slowed by half as he could now only use one finger instead of two. He never progressed to being more than a two-finger typist.

It's easy to see how I inherited my inability to sit and enjoy lunch without feeling the need to work at the same time. I saw Dad do it all too often at the garden centre and for me it's the same today. I use the same two fingers to type as well, if I'm not eating at the same time. Those Hamilton genes strike again!

Needing some information about suppliers of secateurs, Dad ventured over to his filing cabinet and spotted the pile of letters he'd put there earlier. He worked his way through the pile; it was mostly bills, which he immediately filed in the 'to be paid at some point' tray in his office, and returned them to the top of the filing cabinet. These bills came in plain brown envelopes with the relevant company name stamped on the front. There were also a couple of letters in white envelopes with his name and address handwritten; he assumed those were from customers wanting advice. His name and address on the last envelope was typed. As he opened it and pulled out the contents, he saw GARDEN NEWS written in big letters across the top of the sheet of A4 paper.

Dad had learned his lesson with Anglia Television so rather than deciding this was the rejection of the articles he'd been expecting, he decided to remain open-minded about its content. As you do when you don't want to see the actual body of the letter in case it says exactly what you feared, he started by glancing at the bottom of the page to see who it was from. His eyes widened as he saw the signature and underneath he spotted the typed version: Peter Peskett, Editor.

Suddenly in a far greater state of excitement, his eyes pinged straight back to the top of the page where he started to read properly. The letter said that they liked what he had sent and thought their readers would too, so could he send three more articles for them to look at?

Dad didn't need telling twice. February's calendar script was ripped out of the typewriter rollers and a blank sheet of paper inserted. He put his sandwiches to one side and, after one large swig of tea, he was off. It was difficult to get the writing going because all he could think was, '*Garden News* here I come!'.

The boxed calendar was eventually completed but by then Dad was suffering from a situation that plagued him all his self-employed life: he had very little money. This was a big problem because he was in debt to the bank with the mortgage on our house, as well as a small loan for the garden centre. He also owed money to Cyril for the additional loan of money to buy the garden centre. He couldn't borrow any more – but he knew he was onto a winner. He needed to find the extra money to get his gardening calendar printed.

What do you do when you need money? The obvious answer to Dad was to ask Cyril. But he'd already begged and then borrowed a lot of money from Cyril and just couldn't ask again. Instead he managed to persuade his bank manager that he could easily quadruple any investment made. The bank manager was convinced and the money loaned.

The three articles he sent to *Garden News* were as well received as the first two, and a request was made for more. That was fortunate because, as good as the calendars were, they weren't selling at the garden centre. You need to be optimistic to become a horticulturalist, but sometimes this can become unsupported over-optimism.

This lack of return on Dad's and the bank's investment put the future of the garden centre under real pressure. The articles generated income but not enough to cover the running costs. Dad needed the calendars to sell.

His real problem was that he simply wasn't cut out to be a businessman. He was a talented horticulturalist, but when it came to business he wasn't great. This was quite obvious because, even back then, most garden centres had pushed plants further back in their centres in order to sell things that actually made money. Dad wasn't interested in things just to make money; his interest was plants and that's what he focused on, continually telling himself that he just needed to sell enough of them.

This lack of business acumen meant that it wasn't long before the Hamilton Garden Centre closed its doors for the last time. The bank could no longer extend his overdraft, which meant he couldn't pay his creditors.

Chapter 16

The bankruptcy was a massive, life-changing blow for the whole family although ultimately for Dad it turned out to be the best thing that ever happened to him. I'd always thought that the day I was born was his best-ever day, but apparently not!

Dad not only lost his beloved Hamilton Garden Centre, but the house also went as part of the bankruptcy process. With the divorce imminent he was no longer living in the family home by then, so it was Mum and we three boys who were about to become homeless.

There was only one option possible: Mum had to put us on the list for a council house before we were evicted. With the garden centre gone, Dad was in rented accommodation in Lincolnshire where he was earning money by working on the Fens, mainly carrot topping. This work was erratic, so his pay was also unpredictable – as was the money he sent to Mum to help with our upkeep.

Just a week before the cut-off date, a council house in Dorothy Road, Kettering became available and we moved in. I remember the first time I went into the house was the day we moved. Mum had had to accept the first house the council offered, and the overwhelming first impressions were that it was very musty, smelly and in dire need of redecoration.

Still, I was fascinated by the passageway between us and the neighbours. I'd seen this type of structure a lot because many of my schoolfriends lived in this area of Kettering, and I was always envious that their houses had an arched passageway. It's an odd thing to be obsessed with, but then I was an odd boy!

From the word go, the one redeeming factor with this house was that it was half the walk to school; another was that I had plenty of schoolfriends living locally who I could join on that walk.

The first job in the house was to remove the stained wallpaper from every room and redecorate. Mum had acquired a bag of crystals from the local DIY store – I can't remember what brand they were. The instructions said to apply the dissolved crystals to the wallpaper to make removing it easier. I can remember that I needed to wear Marigold gloves and that, once diluted, the solution smelt the same as walking into a gents' toilet. Not just any old gents' toilet but one that hadn't been cleaned for two weeks. This was not my favourite job but we all persevered until the walls were bare. Once scrubbed, we painted them as this was the cheaper option and the only one we could afford with a grant given by the council.

Dad was still working away in the fields in Lincolnshire

and writing articles for *Garden News* in the evenings when they needed them. When he had no work he couldn't send any money. I don't know how Mum managed it, but with innovative cooking and a natural talent with a sewing machine, she always kept us fed and clothed. There were times when she had to be very imaginative with food and buy cheap items from the butcher's – pig's brain, sheep's tongue, any type of offal you care to mention. I used to come home from school to find a big pan on the cooker, lid juddering as the water inside bubbled, and would have an overwhelming urge to see what odd thing was for dinner this time.

I'm not sure if this is a Hamilton or a masculine trait (or both), but I've spent almost every day of my life staggering from one important part of the day to the next. There is no question in my mind that the most important part of the day is any time when food is involved. I love my food. Finding out what was cooking was important because it gave me the perfect incentive to crack on with my least favourite evening entertainment: science homework.

There were times when my love of food was severely tested. I can picture the day I returned from school, removed the lid of the pan on the cooker and was faced with a complete perfectly white brain bubbling in water. Having never seen anything like this before, I didn't know quite what to think of it. I was so concerned that I messed up my science homework ('a little confused' was the teacher's comment at the bottom of the page), as confused as my urge to eat or not. In the end the food turned out all right, although unsurprisingly it was not something I was keen to have again.

That was one of the very few times that I didn't ask for seconds. At the end of meals I would finish anything left on other people's plates. This was not just the case at home but also when we visited Rosa and Cyril, particularly for Sunday lunch.

When cooked *à la* Rosa, Sunday lunch was a feast for twice the number of people attending, which stretched even my eating ability. However, as with everything in my life, I always gave it my best shot, which often resulted in me having to be rolled out to the car.

Because of these humongous efforts, Dad started to call me 'The Human Dustbin'. He often talked about my hollow legs acting as reservoirs for the food that overflowed from my stomach; he was certain that there was no other way that I could consume that quantity of food. I was proud of my title 'The Human Dustbin', but I never ate to maintain it – I ate because I was hungry.

The thing was, I had the physique of an athlete. It fuelled my energetic lifestyle of sports lessons at school, sport in the playground and playing after school. Surely a growing boy needs the energy from plenty of food?

The budget meals Mum concocted were filling and tasty, but the days of the Knickerbocker Glory were long gone. However, I did have a similar experience on a trip to see the mighty Spurs. My friend from school, John Ball, was also a keen Spurs supporter, which was quite surprising as his dad was a Liverpudlian. They lived on the same council estate and close enough for us to regularly meet up to kick a football about.

After one of our regular kickabouts, we popped back to his house for a drink – being only thirteen, it was just a glass of orange squash. We were in his kitchen chatting when his dad strode in and announced that he was going to try and get tickets for the upcoming Tottenham Hotspur versus Brighton & Hove Albion match. Did I want one? I knew Mum couldn't afford it but, before I had the chance to decline, he added that he would treat me to it. He didn't have to ask twice. I was about to be faced with two new experiences: one great, and the other not in the same league of greatness.

My work at school must have suffered considerably during the period between being offered a ticket and the great day coming round. The match was all I could think about. It was the first time I'd been to a proper football match at a big ground like White Hart Lane.

I remember vividly the day when John told me the tickets had arrived. I don't remember what I learned that day, but I definitely recall the tickets arriving. His dad had been round to our house to brief Mum on what was going to happen the following Saturday. He would collect me at 11am and drive all three of us down to London. That would leave plenty of time for a stop on the way down, to find parking and to get into the ground. He'd been to a few top football matches before so he knew the procedure.

When the morning of the match finally arrived, I was ready. I had a blue-and-white scarf, the colours of my team, as well as a stripy bobble hat in the same colours, both knitted for me by Mum. She'd made me a packed lunch, consisting of two cheese-and-pickle sandwiches, a bag of salt-and-vinegar crisps, an apple and a few shop's-own Bourbon-like biscuits. Also in my bag was a bottle of squash.

I was duly collected and the three of us headed south. At no point during the drive down there, the walk to the ground or at any time during the match was I worried about what the score might be. The only thing that really excited me was that I was there. I can't even remember whether Spurs won or lost. The one thing I do remember is that John's dad had somehow managed to get us tickets in the away supporters' end on the tiered seating, so we were totally surrounded by opposition supporters. Randomly, and on more than one occasion, someone shouted 'Seagulls!' Eventually I realised this must be the nickname of Brighton & Hove Albion Football Club. The problem was that when there was an exciting moment from the home team we couldn't join in due to the overwhelming bias of the people around us.

We left the ground and mingled with the supporters we should really have been sitting with who were also heading off home. I doubt too many of the Spurs supporters had the trip we were faced with. It was winter so it was now dark at five o'clock when we spilled out of the ground and onto the surrounding streets. The problem with the dark and an area you're not familiar with is that it becomes difficult to orientate yourself and, apparently, almost impossible to find where you've parked your car. Well, that's what Mr Ball told us.

We wandered up and down several streets for what seemed an eternity, although it was probably only half an hour, before he spotted his bright yellow car. To say it stood out was an understatement. By the time we'd found the car and were ready to set off home, the crowds had dispersed so driving away from the ground wasn't a problem. We tootled along, heading north, and passed very close to my old stomping ground in Hertfordshire before finally getting onto the M1 motorway.

I was starving hungry. It wasn't surprising really, because I'd eaten the entire contents of my lunchbox before we'd got to the end of the M1 motorway on the way down to the match. In the interim I'd not consumed a single thing, not a good situation for a growing boy.

Without warning, Mr Ball turned off the motorway into a service station. I asked where we were going and he replied that, as it was getting late, he was treating me and John to something to eat. Obviously, I immediately thought – Knickerbocker Glory. It's not that I'm obsessed with the joy that is a Knickerbocker Glory, it's just that this was the only food I'd ever consumed at a service station.

Devastatingly a Knickerbocker Glory wasn't on the menu. This wasn't going to be a sit-down food experience, this was grab and go. Apparently Mr Ball had given Mum an idea of the time he was likely to be dropping me off and he didn't want her worrying if we were late. We went into a Wimpy. I'd seen them before because we had one in Kettering, but I'd only walked past and never gone inside.

Mr Ball asked if I liked beefburgers, which I did, and that's exactly what I got: a thin burger between two halves of a bread bun. It took the edge off my hunger, although I did raid the cupboards when I got home. Was this burger better than the pig's brain? I'll let you decide.

Once we reached Dorothy Road, I thanked Mr Ball. I think he knew that I'd had the best time and also experienced two new things in my short life. Mind you, I didn't have to wait long before I returned to the holy place that is White Hart Lane. During the divorce proceedings it was decided that Dad should have his three boys every other weekend. It usually turned out to be just one day rather than the whole weekend because he rented a property that only had one bedroom, although occasionally we stayed at our grandparents' house overnight. Dad always managed to tie that in with an evening meal as an added bonus.

One particular weekend, he'd arranged to pick us up on the Saturday morning. When we got into the car, it was clear that he was excited – almost as excited as we were to see him. Stephen sat in the front, which was his prerogative as the older son, whilst Christopher and I sat in the back.

Dad announced that we were off to the football. I knew he was a Spurs follower, so I don't know why my first thought was that we'd be heading back to Broxbourne to watch the invincible Broxbourne Badgers play on the pitch in the local park. Apparently not; we were off to see Spurs play Aston Villa. I was on my way back to White Hart Lane – and a very happy boy!

Dad had brought supplies and even managed to get tickets for the right end. Again we were in the seated tier, but at the opposite end to where we were seated for the Brighton game. The match had me on the edge of my seat for almost the full ninety minutes. The highlight was the only goal scored by one of the Tottenham Hotspur wingers, Ralph Coates. I remember him collecting the ball in the Spurs half of the pitch and hurtling up the wing with it before firing an unstoppable rocket of a shot into the top left-hand corner of the Aston Villa goal. The goalkeeper had no chance of saving it – I doubt if he even saw it.

However, it wasn't this magnificent strike that I remember the most. Ralph Coates was a footballer with a distinctive hairstyle, a comb-over, which meant that when he was hurtling up the wing, his hair was trailing behind him like the smoke trail of an aeroplane. He was running so fast that the wind made it stick straight out behind his head – fascinating for a teenager.

As with my previous visit to 'The Lane', we arrived back in Kettering quite late. After giving Mum a quick debrief on the game, I settled down to *Match of the Day*. Jimmy Hill was just introducing the Spurs versus Aston Villa match – perfect timing. I watched the match again and it gave me the opportunity to understand that Ralph Coates's hair actually gave the magnificent goal he scored more kudos. It was voted the programme's Goal of the Month, although he didn't even get into the finalists for Hairstyle of the Year.

I was a great admirer of Ralph Coates's speed as he ran with a ball at his feet. Presumably because I was a sprinter at school, but I only just managed to put one foot in front of the other without having to worry about a round thing that I might trip over. My legs might have been short but they whirred as I ran. In fact, I was the second-fastest runner in my year at Henry Gotch; I was only beaten by the boy who ran the 100 and 200 metres for the county. I consoled myself that although he always beat me, I left many others trailing in my wake.

Mind you, athletics wasn't my favourite sport – that was football. Somehow I'd managed to bag the position of left back, not a position where I could use my incredible speed; I thought I'd have been better as a winger. However, Mr Blackwell, the school's head of PE, said that I couldn't cross the ball well enough. Left back turned out to be perfect because it was a position that continually brought out my daredevil streak. I was fearless; there wasn't a tackle that I wouldn't go for. I tackled boys much larger than myself, including those who had a bit of a reputation for aggression in Kettering and beyond.

I'm not sure where this fearless, daredevil streak came from. It certainly wasn't from Dad, who was more of a 'stand back and see what happens first' sort of person. I was generally the first in, not just in football but when I played rugby too. I was still only 4' 11" tall but I would never pull out of tackling a prop forward who looked like a man-mountain. I often repeated the saying 'The bigger they are the harder they fall', knowing that I had much less of a distance to fall.

However, I didn't enjoy all sport. There was one I feared, and that was the dreaded cross-country. This was called sport, but should have come under the heading of modern-day torture. Cross-country sessions always took place in the winter and, for some reason, it always rained.

Henry Gotch School was at the top of a steep hill. First-timers used to charge down the initial descent, not realising that they'd have to complete the ascent at the end. In between was an excessively long course circuit which always involved nettle-filled fields and massive puddles around five-bar gates. We were told to run all the way; if not we wouldn't be showered and changed in time for the start of the next lesson. To make sure we ran, and to spot any cheating, our two PE teachers took turns to follow the students around the course. They were obviously far too smart to run themselves; instead they stood at the top of the hill and followed us using a pair of binoculars.

They had far too good a binocular technique. Many a child was put in detention for not running all the way, while the number of students they caught cheating doesn't bear thinking about. The cheating generally consisted of cutting off parts of the course in order to shorten the distance, although on one of our runs I did notice a boy popping into his house to get nourishment then rejoining us as we passed on the return leg. Needless to say he was spotted and flogged, metaphorically speaking. Hard as it is to believe, there were a couple of students who actually enjoyed this torture, but most of us would have done anything to get out of cross-country running.

I was about to become the envy of all these students. During the previous winter I'd made a terrible error, one that could have ultimately caused my demise at a tender age. Somehow, I'd managed to come in second on a run, and found myself put forward to represent the school in the county cross-country trials. My friend Simon was also selected – he'd staggered in in third place after hanging onto my coat-tails.

Both of us were devastated at the thought of this potentially life-threatening event. Just a few days later I had an appointment to see my heart specialist in Oxford. Was that an opportunity to get medically discharged from this upcoming ordeal?

I was late for my visit to see Dr Gribbin, although it wasn't my fault. As Mum didn't drive, I usually travelled to Oxford in a transport ambulance shared with several other people. There must have been a lack of patients on this particular trip as I was picked up by a taxi driven by a very brusque Scotsman.

Presuming he knew the way, I didn't ask if he'd been to the John Radcliffe Hospital before and I soon discovered that he hadn't. We found ourselves in the centre of Oxford, rather than on the outskirts where the hospital is situated, surrounded by lots of university students on bicycles. Unable to find his way out, the driver resorted to winding down his window and shouting obscenities at them. All the students seemed totally unfazed by these outbursts, so I assumed they were regular occurrences as they cycled around the city.

When I eventually got to the hospital to see Dr Gribbin, he asked if I was feeling well, which I was. Knowing that I was in all the school teams, he asked if I was coping all right with sport at school. I said that I was, but occasionally I felt a little light-headed. He quizzed me and I saw my opportunity. I actually had felt light-headed as I ran back up the hill to school after the cross-country run, so I wasn't lying when I told him that. I hoped that this would instigate my freedom pass, but nothing was forthcoming. He just wrote lots of words on a piece of paper in my file. He didn't seem concerned. It seemed that I was destined to run.

Simon and I spent the next two weeks plotting the best way to extricate ourselves from the cross-country team. The only thing we came up with was to be ill on the day. The run was to be on the following Saturday. According to our PE teachers, this timing was excellent because we could slot in a practice run during our last PE lesson three days before the event.

While we were changing into our running gear, I noticed that only one teacher was present. We waited for Mr Blackwell to appear and take us to the start of the run. The door opened and in he strode clutching a piece of paper. He called out my surname and beckoned me over. With everyone watching, I walked that lonely trail like a convict to the executioner's block. I felt sure that he had discovered our plot to avoid the weekend's race.

Mr Blackwell took me into his office, sat me down and read the letter he was clutching. It was from Dr Gribbin and it excused me from *all* cross-country running at school. I'll repeat that: it excused me from *all* cross-country running! I was so overjoyed I nearly burst. I was so excited at this pardon that I wanted to jump up and down. In the end, I'd pulled it off and the doctor had come good.

There was no mention of excluding me from any other sport, so I could continue to represent my form and my school in every 'short-distance' sport. I returned to my seat and stayed put as all the other boys went out into the cold and damp for their exhausting run. They all looked at me, wondering how I'd managed to escape the punishment. When they got back, I filled them in on my lucky escape.

I was the envy of my whole year group. I was excused from the upcoming county trial, and Simon followed through on our plan and didn't turn up on Saturday morning. Returning to school on Monday, nobody demanded to see him about his no-show so he thought he'd got away with it. He decided he'd mention to a PE teacher during our PE lesson next day that he'd been under the weather and couldn't run. This he did. Mr Blackwell was fair, but was also firm with anyone who stepped out of line. The story didn't wash with him and his 'no-run' cross-country punishments showed that: Simon was banned from playing football in PE lessons or for the school team for the next five weeks. Instead, he was made to run round the football pitch while we played. Needless to say, Simon was never ill again.

Now I was able to concentrate on my burgeoning football and rugby careers. My school team football experiences hadn't started in the most encouraging way for a budding football great. Dad was always very encouraging about my sporting pursuits; I'm not sure if that was because he saw potential or because they wore me out. He even found positive words when I arrived home after a 21–0 drubbing by a local school football team.

I was in my first year at secondary school and this was my first experience of being in a school sports team. We weren't very good, but we did run round a lot and tried our hardest. This particular match was against a team from Our Lady's School, Corby, a terrifying prospect because of the inevitable rivalry between teams from towns in such close proximity. Also, all the school football teams in Corby were always much better than we were.

We hadn't played football on their pitch before this fateful day, so we weren't prepared for their unusual playing surface. We arrived at the school and were directed to the dressing room, where we changed into our kit and trotted out. The pitch was located some distance away. After the match, as we were travelling home in the coach, the consensus was that this was a definite ploy to wear us out before the match started because it took quite a lot of running around to locate it.

When we arrived, we couldn't believe our eyes – the pitch was on an almost forty-five-degree slope! Going from the bottom goal up to the top one was like climbing the north face of the Eiger!

We won the toss and, after a quick discussion, we felt that our best ploy was to kick downhill during the first half to get as far ahead as we could. This would obviously demoralise the opposition so, come the second half, we could hang onto our lead and walk away the winners. It was a bold plan because winning wasn't something we had ever experienced before. If only we'd known what they said about 'the best-laid plans'.

By half-time, we were 12–0 down. According to the teacher, who was also our coach, we'd done well to keep the score down to that. Did he say that because they'd been superlative in the first half, or because we were so bad?

I had gained a reputation for being a prolific goalscorer and had scored some goals that would definitely have made Goal of the Month on *Match of the Day*. The only problem with this ability to score prolifically was that I played at left back and all my goals had been in the wrong goal; they were all own goals. I managed to score in the first half of this game too, although it was just a deflection that I couldn't get out of the way of.

There aren't many footballers who come out for the second half determined not to score, but that was my aim. Our second-half performance was staggering; we only conceded nine goals and the opposition were kicking downhill. Most surprising of all, during the full forty-five minutes I managed not to add to my own goal tally.

Dad's comment was that there were always going to be better teams than us, and the most important thing was to make sure that next time we lost by a smaller margin. When we played Our Lady's the following year, we only lost 4–1. Not only did we manage to concede just four goals, but we scored. I was as proud as Punch too, and even prouder not to have scored an own goal this time.

The problem I faced was that my ability to score goals past our own goalkeeper had become legendary. When it happened I just had to accept it and laugh about it. At the end of the day it was a school football team, so there wasn't a lot riding on the result, only pride, and we weren't good enough to have much of that.

A lot of the goals I netted were similar to the one against Our Lady's, in that I had little control when a ball was kicked directly at me and it just bounced off into the goal. There seemed to be a disproportionate number of shots that would hit me on their way towards the goal. That said, I also scored some absolute beauties. These were met with much more excitement.

The best goal I scored generated both pride and fear. The ball was passed to me by one of our centre backs and, as it approached, I saw one of their team bearing down on me. My immediate – and correct – thought was to pass the ball back to our goalkeeper because, in those days, he could pick it up from a back pass. The problem was that the ball hit some mud as I went to kick it and flew majestically into the top right-hand corner of our goal. The goalkeeper flew full length towards it but only managed to grasp thin air. It even had a bit of curl on it, which amazed and pleased me in equal measure as this was something I'd never managed before (or since).

As the goalkeeper collected the ball from the back of the net, I smiled in wonder at the quality of the goal I'd scored, albeit in the wrong goal. At this point I was approached by one of our midfielders, a lad called Steve, who I assumed had trotted over to me to congratulate me on my spectacular effort. Unfortunately not; he was a boy of few words and only came over to tell me that if I laughed again when I scored an own goal, he would punch my lights out. Very thoughtful.

My football started at a low standard and improved as I went through school, but my other sporting activities had a bit more of a bumpy ride. I was picked for the gymnastics display on school sports day, in addition to running the 100 and 200 metres sprints and the 100 metres hurdles in the inter-form competition. I didn't know it at the time, but this would turn out to be a *dies horribilis.*

As usual, I'd come second in both sprints and I was more than happy with that. I really didn't want to run in the next event. It took a lot of effort to get within shouting distance of the newly crowned county 100 metres champion and the hurdles were very high. It took a great leap just to clear one, let alone ten. I knew that the combination of sprinting and leaping was a recipe for disaster. According to the rest of my form, however, I was the best of all of them at hurdles and someone had already put my name on the entry form.

I lined up at the start line with the other seven racers. Off went the starter's pistol and I set off at full speed. I hit the first hurdle with such force that my balance went completely and I ended up stuck face first in a muddy grass field. I lifted my head to check if I was the only prostrate figure on the track; I was.

To add insult to injury, I remembered that the straight sprint track was just below the school playground which doubled as the perfect viewing platform, so my acrobatic dive was witnessed by virtually the whole school.

I dusted myself down, removed as much of the mud

as possible, and headed off to the centre of the sports field. By the time I arrived at the gymnastics apparatus, I was feeling less of a hurdling idiot and more like a professional gymnast. In hindsight, this may have been the problem. I was confident because Mr Blackwell had told the whole group that I was one of the school's best gymnasts and an excellent vaulter. The vaulting horse had been set up with a mini trampette placed at one end. The whole display was to start with a simple manoeuvre that we'd performed during PE lessons so many times that I could do in my sleep.

Each gymnast had to fly through the air and land with their hands on either side of the horse, as close to the end as possible. The momentum took you into a handstand and then you pushed off to land on your feet, arms in the air. This was a fluidly continuous piece of gymnastics.

The events became more complicated after that. Once everyone had completed the first manoeuvre, we would all go again but this time with a half-twist. For the big finale, another trampette was bought out and placed in the middle of the long side of the vaulting horse so that we could carry out the handstand push off but with two lines of gymnasts crossing in an alternate fashion.

Not only did we still have the whole school watching, but we also had a crowd of parents, Mum included, for this spectacular end to our sports day. I was performing last each time and executed the first two manoeuvres perfectly. We then waited the two minutes it took for the second trampette to be put into place. At the last moment, Mr Blackwell decided that it had gone so well that we would do this final manoeuvre twice; once we had landed, we were to run back and join the line, ready to go again.

My first attempt at this final vault combination came and went perfectly. I went back to the line, knowing I'd be the last to fly through the air. I was so pumped up for this big finish that the second time I hurtled towards the trampette as fast as I could, adrenalin pumping. I completely forgot about the control element of gymnastics and hit the trampette with such force that I was catapulted into the air at a speed that made my eyes water. I stretched out into a flying-swan pose and flew majestically through the air. I saw the end of the vaulting horse come and go and suddenly the padded mat came into view. I landed in the same flying-swan position, yet again face-first. Twice in one day was an achievement in itself. I rose to a combination of giggles and rousing applause.

The next time Dad collected us for his weekend, I recounted the sports day events. He approached each event individually and his evaluation was simple. Firstly, it was a ridiculous idea to put obstacles in the way of sprinters; why would you want to slow sprinters down by putting up hurdles? My thoughts exactly. Secondly, had anyone else been able to fly that far through the air? No, of course not. At no point did he mention that I was supposed to land on the end of the vaulting horse, he just focused on how far I managed to propel myself.

I was fourteen and realised that he was being kind and encouraging, but it helped me to avoid dwelling on the incident, particularly when he finished by telling me that I was undoubtedly the only Henry Gotch Secondary School pupil ever to land twice on my face during a single sports day. I was in fact a record holder.

Chapter 17

While we were still living in Wormley, and once both Stephen and I could reach the dining table, Dad decided that we needed to help around the house. Every day he would arrive home just in time for dinner. This meant that Mum had to look after three young boys while trying to create a culinary masterpiece to put on the table, which was easier on some days than others. Dad decided that the responsibility of helping around the home should fall on my and Stephen's shoulders.

We gladly accepted this new responsibility because it helped make sure that dinner ran smoothly. Stephen and I alternated weekly with the responsibility of laying the table. That meant not only getting out the cutlery but laying it in the right order and, most importantly of all, making sure that five places were set.

This task was so important that it was given the name of 'Service'. No matter what else was occurring, we would carry out Service whenever the food was nearly ready. On rare occasions that meant missing part of John Craven's *Newsround*. That verged on the criminal – how could any parent subject their children to such a sacrifice?

Eventually, the joyful day came when Christopher could also reach the dining table so our Service commitment went from bi-weekly to once every three weeks. Even at such an early age, we knew that life is full of significant little moments that need celebrating.

Dad was inspired by his new naming system. Out of the blue, he announced that his three sons should now address him as 'Your Holiness'. This affected every part of our lives. We had only known one way to behave at the table for breakfast, lunch and dinner: when we had finished eating, we had to wait for everyone else to finish and only then could we ask to get down from the table.

Now we were only allowed to leave the table once we'd asked in the correct manner: 'Can I get down from the table please, Your Holiness?' Dad's new rule affected everything: 'Can we go outside please, Your Holiness?', 'Can I have a biscuit please, Your Holiness?', 'Did you want to play Monopoly, Your Holiness?' You get the idea.

This continued for months, until the day His Holiness took Stephen with him to the newsagent's to collect his Sunday paper. It was peak time for newspaper collection and the newsagent's was packed. After getting his paper, Dad joined the queue to pay while Stephen amused himself by looking at the comics laid out on the bottom shelf.

He started to read a particularly funny edition of

The Beano and thought that it would be something his brothers would enjoy too. Comics were not something we often received except at Christmas, when they formed part of our Christmas stockings. Not only did we enjoy them but they stopped us waking Dad up too early.

He took *The Beano* to Dad, who was still waiting in the long queue. When he arrived he asked, 'Could I please have this comic, Your Holiness?'

It was as if the world just stopped. The shop went quiet and everyone turned round to look at Stephen then glared at Dad. Strangely, we weren't encouraged to call him this ever again.

Even though he'd moved away from his papal position, Dad hadn't finished with his sayings. It didn't take long for anyone, his children included, to understand that he would use (what he considered to be) a funny saying whenever possible. When each of us became a teenager, he employed a very popular saying whenever and wherever he could: 'It's because you'll never be the man that I am.' He'd say it when something didn't go according to plan or one of us didn't know how to get something started.

This saying wasn't just reserved for projects; it even found its place in games and other innocuous activities, such as felling a coconut at the fair, pinning the tail on the donkey and even balancing a 1p coin on its narrow edge on your chin. When we failed at any task and he stepped in, or did it first time, we'd ask how he managed it when we couldn't. The answer was always the same – 'It's because you'll never be the man that I am.'

As a young child, I interpreted this to mean 'you'll be able to do it when you become a dad, because this is what dads can do'. As I've aged, I realised that's exactly what he meant – although becoming a dad certainly didn't guarantee success. Had I taken his words the wrong way, it could have scarred me for life. I know Dad meant it to be funny, but in hindsight he was treading a very fine line.

Saying that, he never used put-downs and was very encouraging even in the most dire situations. Obviously there were times when irritation took over. Like most people, he could ignore something annoying for a period of time, hoping it would change or go away, but if it didn't he'd get to the point where he needed to comment – even if it probably wouldn't make any difference.

From a very early age, I've always frowned. This wasn't because I was upset or annoyed, it was either while I was concentrating or when I was captivated by something, but it unnerved Dad. I'm not sure why, but he used to comment on it regularly. As I got older, this comment began to acquire a more irritated tone. He just couldn't understand why I frowned. He feared that people who weren't aware of my unusual trait would get the wrong impression and I might not make friends easily or get on in business. This was another 'rhubarb' moment. One where he just couldn't – or wouldn't – understand that I had no control over what was happening.

Fortunately in the case of one of my other major flaws, it wasn't Dad who suffered most but Mum. I had an uncanny ability to get dirty. Whatever I did and wherever I went, I seemed to be in a permanent state of muddiness. It didn't make any difference if I'd been to the rowing club, the garden centre, fishing, on a visit to the grandparents or going to Saturday (Sunday) school – I would come home covered in mud. There were days when it would have been easier to hose me down rather than putting my clothes in the washing machine.

Dad finally managed just one exasperated comment: 'I don't know how you do it. Do you just stand still and mud hurls itself at you?' I don't think he ever realised how close to the truth he was and that this ability would continue right through my life, even when I was trying really hard to stay clean.

For someone who was so encouraging to anyone trying something new or interesting, it was surprising when occasionally Dad went out of his way to actively discourage. The prime example was with his own dad, Cyril.

Cyril and Rosa only had one car and a double garage. Rosa was always on the prowl for things that needed adjusting and tweaking to improve her social standing. For her, having a half-empty garage didn't sit well as all their middle-class friends would have turned unused garage space into a workshop. Cyril, therefore, had to purchase a full range of woodworking tools to add to those he already had and create a workshop.

The garage was a deluxe model and the workshop didn't fill it all so, in desperation, Cyril felt he needed to find a hobby before Rosa found one for him. Fortunately for him, he had a friend who was dabbling in winemaking. This was just what Cyril was looking for. He liked wine, so why not make his own? He knew that this hobby, although alcohol-related, would pass the Rosa middle-class test – he'd never have got away with home-brew beer.

Dad was pleased for him because it gave Cyril something to do that he really did enjoy. Every time their garage door opened, I thought it looked like a moonshine distillery. I'd never come across glass demi-john jars before, let alone all the other winemaking gear. Typically, Cyril had all the kit he needed and quite a lot he'd never use, but it looked impressive.

Dad encouraged his dad in his newfound hobby until the first gallon of wine was ready to drink. As he took the first mouthful Dad realised that, although Cyril really enjoyed it making wine, he wasn't very good at it. When asked his opinion, Dad lied and said that it was a good first attempt. Unintentionally, this spurred Cyril on.

It wasn't long before there was enough wine being produced for it to be offered to Dad every time we went round for Sunday lunch or just popped in to visit. However, Mum had managed to get out of drinking it, by claiming that she was teetotal. Cyril never asked how come a French woman didn't drink wine, and Mum never elaborated. One strange result of Cyril's winemaking was the rapid growth of the potted houseplants, as Dad watered them. It's not a documented way of caring for your houseplants, but they grew well when fed wine. This continued for a couple of years. That was unusual for Dad; normally he'd have found a way out more quickly.

One Sunday we pulled onto our grandparents' drive. As we got out of the car, I noticed that Dad had a bottle in his hand. I asked why and was just told that it was a present for Grandpa. As we entered the bungalow he presented it to Cyril, who didn't notice the massive smile on Dad's face. Grandpa asked why he'd brought this bottle when there was a perfectly good elderberry wine in the garage. Dad's reply came very quickly and firmly: 'Oh well, we'll drink this one now that I've brought it.'

This game continued every time we visited until the day Cyril died. Dad then ensured that Rosa gave away as much of Cyril's winemaking kit as possible, making a point of including the demijohns already filled with wine. The last thing Dad needed was for this wine nightmare to continue. He had thousands of fantastic memories of his dad, which didn't need tainting by the demon demijohns.

I'm sure Cyril worked out Dad's little game, and that it was he who decided to get Rosa a knitting machine as a means of reprisal. As a teenager, I'd already received the birthday present from Rosa and

Cyril of a shirt that looked like the top half of a pair of pyjamas and was therefore only wearable when we visited our grandparents. That was followed by the Christmas present after Rosa mastered her newfangled knitting machine. She was knocking out baby clothes for her friends' grandchildren, jumpers for Cyril and her friends' husbands – but greater things were in the offing. She had a plan and nothing was going to divert her from her chosen path.

That Christmas each of us, including Dad but not Mum, received a present of the same dimensions, each one wrapped in the same Christmas wrapping paper. Rosa saved them so we could open them when we went round to their house on Christmas Day afternoon. One by one we were handed our presents, and one by one we pulled out a black polo neck jumper. That was useful when we all lived in the same house. As you do, particularly at your grandparents, we all said the same thank you and pretended we were delighted at getting something we really wanted.

Once they'd all been opened and polo necks displayed, Cyril saw his opportunity and suggested that we should try them on to see if they fitted. He was going for the jugular so that his winemaking revenge would be complete. He had undoubtedly had a jumper made from the same wool, so he knew exactly what he was doing.

All four of us pulled our jumpers over our heads. My problem was the size of my head and the size of the neck of the jumper; Rosa was well aware that I had a large cranium but hadn't allowed for it while she was sliding the carriage up and down her machine and knocking out these woollen masterpieces. By the time I'd managed to ease through my head, the others were already showing the surrounding crowd of three (Mum, Rosa and Cyril) how great they looked.

As my head popped out I caught a glimpse of Stephen scratching an itch on his neck and I realised why. She'd made all four of them with the same wool, which must have been the itchiest available. Cyril's smile was not one of pleasure, generated by seeing his son and three grandchildren looking like they'd just arrived from the Paris catwalk; it was definitely a smirk of satisfaction. His revenge was complete. All four polo neck sweaters went into cupboards at home and were only aired on winter visits to the top fashion nutter – sorry knitter – and her vengeful husband.

I have to admit that my fashion sense never recovered from this experience. My whole life I've been about three years behind everyone else when it came to being fashionable; at least, that's how other people have viewed it. I've always thought that I was way ahead of my time.

There's a genetic reason for that, too: Dad. He was as far removed as a follower of fashion as Cyril was with his garage full of wine from Dom Pérignon in the cellars of Moët & Chandon. Trying to explain how fashionable he was during his teenage and young adult life, he told me was that there were the mods, the rockers and the baggy-jumper brigade. He asked me to guess which fashion faction he'd belonged to. That wasn't the hardest question I ever had to answer; when working outside in winter, you can get more items of clothing under a baggy jumper. It was always more about the practicalities.

Chapter 18

Dad's daily grind continued for a while longer until his big break came. He was starting to wonder whether his career as a part-time journalist was going to lead anywhere when, out of the blue, a writer left *Garden News* and he was asked to fill in on a full-time contract. This wasn't just a relief to him, his career path, his wallet and therefore to us, but also to his back, which had really taken a hammering after being bent double all day, every day harvesting veg in the fields of Lincolnshire.

During his time as a part-time contributor with *Garden News*, he had worked well with both Peter Peskett and Geoff Amos, so his transition to full-time journalism was seamless. He took to it as if he'd been born to it. As well as writing articles for the paper, he provided copy for the back-page regular column, called *The Last Word*. He loved writing that column because he could write whatever he wanted as long as it had a vague horticultural connection.

Dad wasn't opinionated but he did like to push boundaries, and he covered topics nobody had thought of or would have dared write about. On occasion, he might upset a company or organisation with his comments but, as they were truthful and needed saying to bring the problem to the public's attention, he felt this was his duty. As he saw it, some things needed highlighting. If people didn't like the truth being written about them and what they did, or about their products, then so be it; that was their problem, not his.

He went from strength to strength. Readers loved not only the subjects he was covering, including *The Last Word*, but also his easy-to-read style. This success with the readership didn't go unnoticed; a couple of years later, when the editor of *Practical Gardening* left his post, Dad was asked if he would like to become the magazine's new editor. He was flabbergasted by the request, and excited and nervous in equal degrees at the thought of this promotion. Being daunted was understandable as *Practical Gardening* was the top monthly gardening magazine at the time. It was owned by East Midlands Allied Press (EMAP), the company that also owned *Garden News*, and was based in the same building. Dad was so proud to be the editor and to have his own office with his name on the door, but it was a bittersweet pill for him to swallow because he was still working in Peterborough.

The relationships he had built within EMAP helped massively with this new and very exciting project, but he really didn't like working in the city and would have preferred to be based in a more rural setting. For his job this really wasn't an option, so he decided that a home in the countryside was what he needed to balance out the days spent in the city.

I think Rosa must have helped massively in his search for the ideal cottage by stepping in and getting on her direct line to 'Him upstairs' (apparently posh people can do that). Surprise, surprise: Dad stumbled across a cottage for rent in rural Rutland. It was in the countryside and Dad jumped at the opportunity to move in.

The first time I visited Dad there, I remember that I was late. That wasn't because I hadn't left enough time to get to his new abode on my Suzuki AP50 moped, but because I spent at least half an hour trying to find his residence amongst all the other buildings. His new cottage was part of the old stable block at Barnsdale Hall. The Hall was located about a mile and a half from the villages of Exton to the north, Whitwell to the east and the county town of Oakham two miles to the west. When I eventually found it, his part of the stable block was tucked away in the corner of a walled, rectangular courtyard.

After spending a further ten minutes trying to get in, I had to virtually break down the badly fitting door. My first impression was that it was dark, dingy and very sparsely furnished. The darkness and dinginess were not something he wanted but were all his budget would allow in Rutland. But the lack of furniture, ornaments, curtains, etc., wasn't a problem as long as he had a garden.

A garden wasn't part of the original deal he'd made when renting this small part of the stable block, so he put his name down for an allotment in Oakham. Never one to miss an opportunity, however, he noticed that there was some land at the end of the very bumpy dirt track that was jokingly called his drive. It was a fairly steep drive and at the top this plot was not being used for anything. The surrounding fields were used to graze sheep, but this bit was in an awkward place and overgrown with weeds. It was situated between two workshops used for respraying cars, and to the side of a double cottage. He knew instantly that it was just what he was looking for and he started to make a plan.

Barnsdale Hall was owned by the Dickinson family, a mother and her grown-up children. Dad became friendly with Jim Dickinson and it was Jim's car-spraying workshop that stood in front of Dad's potential new garden. It was Jim who introduced Dad to the joys of the Noel Arms in Whitwell, the closest place locally to wet your whistle and they often met there for a swift half of Ruddles County Ale.

One evening, being the opportunist he was, Dad engineered the conversation round to the wasteland. Jim was also one never to miss an opportunity, particularly if it would generate income, and a week later Dad was offered the two acres of wasteland for a very reasonable rent. That was Jim's description of the rent, not Dad's.

The first job was to clear the weeds so that Dad could see what lay beneath and, most importantly what the soil was like. He was fascinated with old horticultural tools and equipment and had an old scythe in an outbuilding next to his cottage, which was perfect for the weed clearing. Luckily nobody saw his first attempts, which looked more like an Olympic hammer thrower limbering up, but after a while he managed to get into the rhythm of scything and after a few days the tops of the weeds were no more.

Dad's intention was to dig out the perennial weeds and as he began to dig up the long taproot weeds, he quickly realised that he was renting two acres of heavy clay.

His plan for the plot was to create a bed for growing cut flowers and use the remainder for vegetables, fruit trees and fruit bushes. He didn't just want to grow produce for himself; his primary objective was to make sure the fruit and veg content in *Practical Gardening* magazine was improved. He knew there were plenty of people out there who didn't realise they could be vegetable gardeners, and he wanted to encourage them to start and follow him in his new venture. Consequently, not only did he have a non-stop supply of fruit and veg but he also generated pictures and features for the magazine.

Unquestionably one of his greatest purchases was his second-hand Howard Gem rotavator. This orange beast could chop through any ground, weeded or not, as well as prepare seedbeds where the soil needed to be finely chopped. When Dad had carried out his national service, the drill sergeant had told them all that their rifle was their best friend and they were to treat it as such; there is no doubt that Howard the Rotavator surpassed this status in Dad's life. I'm sure that if Dad could have got this machine up the stairs, he'd have gone to bed with it.

I had used a Howard Gem rotavator when I worked at the Lea Valley Horticultural Experimental Station in Hertfordshire during my year's industry experience prior to going to Writtle College. It always makes me smile when I hear people talking about rotavating the ground instead of digging because it will be easier. This monster took muscles to control, and even a short stint made you lose gallons of sweat. Not only did it do a fantastic job at cultivating the ground, it certainly kept you fit and trim.

In the horticultural world they were known to have two great assets: the first was their legendary ability to rotavate any ground; the second was that if anything fell off it or looked precarious, it could easily be tied back on with baler twine without hindering its purpose. For years it has been virtually impossible to come across one without at least part of it attached with twine; some gardeners felt that they weren't authentic or didn't run properly unless they had bits tied on with twine. It exemplified the gardening philosophy of 'make do and mend'.

Once he'd removed the perennial weeds and given the full two acres a once-over with the Howard Gem, it was time to start laying out the veg beds. While writing an article for *Garden News*, Dad had visited a keen amateur veg grower who grew everything in four-foot-wide raised beds. Obviously Dad knew about this way of growing but he'd never had the opportunity to try it out for himself. As he did with any new idea he came across during his horticultural career, he experimented first by growing some veg in beds and some in traditional, straight rows. He didn't want to install permanent beds in case he decided the system was not for him and he'd have to dismantle them again. Instead he marked out three four-foot-wide beds and double-dug each one, leaving a path measuring about a foot across between them. Double-digging and adding a good amount of well-rotted horse manure raised the soil quite a lot and he was happy with the outcome. He then sowed and planted different veg into each bed, as well as in rows, using the same varieties for both so that he had a direct comparison.

Not content with having these outside crops, he set his sights on more exotic veg and, during the first season, he managed to blag a couple of ten-by-thirty-foot polythene tunnels from a renowned tunnel maker. These were going to be a great addition to his articles for the magazine, so he promised the manufacturer that the magazine would follow a tunnel-grown crop through its growing season. Dad often teased Rosa that he had chutzpah because of the family's Jewish heritage, particularly when it came to blagging things. He may have used this term in a light-hearted manner but, when it came to blagging, chutzpah it certainly was.

The tunnels proved a great asset for propagation, as well as for growing early protected crops such as tomatoes, cucumbers, melons, peppers, aubergines and a whole host of winter salad crops. The two-acre area of growing land was now full. The bed system worked really well so Dad expanded it, although he still kept growing in rows so that his readers could see both methods at work.

What he needed in order to maximise the benefits for *Practical Gardening* magazine was an area for growing ornamental plants, preferably in a residential situation. This wasn't possible in the stable block as there was no available land around it. There was a driveway, a cobbled courtyard and trees surrounding his cottage, but no bare soil.

While gardening his plot he would spend time gazing at the double-fronted red-brick cottage just next door. If it hadn't been opposite Jim Dickinson's car-spraying workshop, it would have been an idyllic place for him to live. However, he thought it was still better for his purposes than the stable-block cottage. Not only was it next door to his plot, meaning that he could step out of his back door and be gardening within ten paces, but it also had a garden area which he could use for growing ornamental plants.

His one problem was that it was occupied. I recently heard a talk given by Uri Geller where he spoke about the power of the mind. I'm not sure if Dad used this technique, or whether it was just one of life's coincidences, but without warning the group of young people living in the cottage moved on to pastures new. The day they moved, Dad had Jim pinned in his workshop and wouldn't let him leave until an agreement had been achieved. Dad was now the proud renter of a double red-brick cottage.

When it was time to move on up the hill, he asked me to help. I wasn't sure why because it only took two trips in his Ford Granada Estate to move from one house to the other. I laughed as I told him how sad it was that all he owned fitted into two Ford Granada Estates. Later, when I went to college, I got all of my possessions into a Hillman Imp. Needless to say I never mentioned this to Dad.

It was only after we had emptied the final load that his cunning plan became obvious. It wasn't the move he needed help with but weeding the garden around the cottage. I got a distinct feeling of *déjà vu*, having helped with digging out perennial weeds on the first plot.

Once I'd left, Dad continued with the weed removal until he got to the point where he was ready to plant. The trees went in first, then the shrubs and perennials, and the gaps were filled with annuals. The annuals were needed to make the garden look more mature and fuller than it was for the sake of the photos for the magazine. He had a great first growing season, as his very floriferous ornamental garden started to take on a very cottagey feel, while any allotment holder would have been proud of this fully productive two acres.

Having said that, there were a few odd events in what was, to his readership, now known as Barnsdale. The most memorable of these occurred on a warm, sunny Friday in late March 1980. I was studying for A levels at Kettering Technical College but had no lectures on that day, so rather than go in to to study in the library, I pootled up to Barnsdale on my moped to see Dad.

When I arrived he wasn't in the house, so I left my helmet and gloves on the kitchen table and ventured outside to find him. I knew where he'd be and headed off towards his productive area. As I approached, I saw him in the distance bent over one of his raised beds with someone messing about with equipment next to him. As I got closer, I realised that this was none other than the EMAP photographer, Rod Sloane, and he was setting up his camera and tripod.

Dad was taking butterhead lettuces out of plastic bags, similar to the ones you find in supermarkets. Once each lettuce had been removed from the bag it was placed carefully on the ground, equally spaced, cut end down. I was confused and asked what he was doing. It seemed that they were running a feature on salad crops in the June issue of *Practical Gardening* and the front cover was going to be a lovely picture of harvesting home-grown lettuce. They'd scoured their library of photos, only to find that there were no suitable stock pictures so they were left with no option but to take one themselves.

OK, I could understand that, but why was he not

taking a picture of his own lettuce? Apparently, Dad's winter lettuce weren't good enough for a front-cover picture. It had been a fairly hard winter, so maybe there was too much browning on the edges of the leaves.

I asked where the lettuce he was carefully placing on the ground came from. As if stating the obvious, he said, 'The Co-op.'

So Dad was taking lettuce bought from the Co-op out of bags and placing them on the ground so that he could fake a picture of harvesting home-grown lettuce, which would then go on the front cover of the best-selling gardening magazine in the country. There was only one thing I could say.

'You can't do that!' I blurted out.

'Why not?' he replied. 'No one will ever know.' And, of course, no one ever did.

The problem with monthly magazines was that the pictures and text had to be ready three months prior to the publication date because they had to be printed and sent to subscribers a month early. If you didn't have a suitable picture in March for the June issue, what other option did you have?

Dad couldn't bring himself to actually eat a shop-bought lettuce, so Rod went home with a dozen butterhead lettuce for his family and friends, while Dad went and harvested himself a so-called substandard winter lettuce from another raised bed. Even though in the early days at Barnsdale he wasn't a hundred per cent organic, he was well aware of the difference in quality and flavour between home-grown and shop-bought produce.

Chapter 19

He certainly wasn't worried about quality when he bought my first car. This one was all about price, and Dad knew that when it came to cars Jim Dickinson was prepared to strike a deal. Not only did Jim respray vehicles of all types, he also dabbled in buying and selling used cars and vans.

Unknown to me, Dad had already spoken about the sort of car he wanted for me but, more importantly, how much he was prepared to pay. My first car turned out to be a black Austin Morris 1300. Well, it had to be. At the time of its purchase, I had just started to take driving lessons so it was kept outside Dad's house at Barnsdale. This was because I was working at the Experimental Horticultural Station in Hertfordshire, but I went home each weekend. After racing up to Barnsdale on my moped, I would drive my Austin Morris round the tracks in and around the house, as well as up and down the hill. All private land, of course.

I loved that car, not just because it reignited all those childhood memories, apart from being carsick, but because it had a green flashing light at the end of the indicator stick. How cool was that? I didn't need to indicate because I wasn't on the road, but why wouldn't you if you had such a fantastic green flashing light?

Perfect as this car was, when Dad bought it Jim had told him that it needed an MOT. He'd given it the once-over and it was fine, so no problem. The MOT was due three weeks before my driving test – and it failed! Jim was an expert when it came to respraying, but obviously not when it came to the roadworthiness of motor vehicles.

The list of failings was so long the report should just have said 'this car belongs on the scrap heap', because that's where it ended up. The next car was a Datsun Cherry 100A in bright red. Not to be deterred by the first car failing, this was also a Jim Dickinson purchase, but this one went like a rocket and it had a valid MOT. It served me well during my first year at horticultural college, getting me there and back and ferrying me and several college friends around Essex.

The car was of an age where things start to rattle when you hit 60mph. If you ever got close to 80mph with no police on the horizon, things started to fly off. So when on my way home for a weekend visit I heard a very strange noise from under the bonnet, I didn't initially think anything of it. To be fair, I'd been tanking along the A414 so I should have really been expecting it.

After several miles, and even after slowing down, the noise didn't go away. I pulled over, lifted the bonnet to have a look but couldn't see anything. Not being particularly gifted in the mechanical knowledge department, I thought it might be the brakes. That turned out to be an inspired thought, not because it was anything to do with the brakes but because when I checked the brake behind my left front wheel, I noticed the suspension was almost rubbing on the wheel itself.

When I followed the spring upwards, it was clear what had happened: the mounting had given way and was attached to the car by the thinnest shred of metal. Even I could tell this wasn't normal. What was I to do? I was on a busy trunk road with no roadside assistance cover. Obviously I did what all decent horticultural students would do – got into the car and carried on.

I did have a moment of sensible thinking in that I decided that it wasn't prudent to stay on the A1 in case the suspension decided to part company with the car. The cost of being towed off a major trunk road didn't even bear thinking about. After checking my road map, I set off again. Things were going well, in that the car was still moving forwards.

I tootled around a never-ending bend in the road and onto a straight stretch of carriageway and saw a very long lay-by in the distance. I wondered whether I should stop and check the suspension, but was put off from doing this by two things. Firstly, I was concerned that if I stopped the car from its current forward momentum it might decide not to move again. Secondly, and rather strangely, there was a car parked in the lay-by and what I assumed was its occupant was standing on the side of the road looking towards the oncoming traffic. Had he broken down and thus looking for assistance? His head was turned towards the oncoming traffic. That meant he was either looking at me or the car rapidly approaching from my rear.

Suddenly I found my heart in my mouth and beads of sweat appearing on my brow. Surely the suspension hadn't given way? No, it was worse than that. The car in the lay-by was a police car and the lone figure standing at the side of the road was a policeman.

I knew my car was not in what you'd class as a roadworthy condition and then I suddenly remembered that it was being run as a student car – not taxed either!

What to do? I glanced around for ideas, but there was no emergency exit, no small country lane to divert on to, and doing a U-turn would seem a rather obvious means of avoiding him. I was left with just the one option, to continue driving and take my chances.

I was ready with my defence: I was driving such a rattletrap because I was a very poor horticulture student and was struggling to survive on the meagre support I was receiving. It's true, I was receiving a full grant from Northamptonshire County Council because I was living with Mum. Being a single parent and only working part-time, she didn't earn enough for her income to have a negative impact on my grant. The big problem was that each individual council set its own grant limits – and my grant just covered the cost of tuition fees, accommodation, lunch and evening meal.

There was nothing left to buy textbooks or, God forbid, for a bit of entertainment.

This postcode lottery for awarding grants seemed unfair. Even more sickening was that the friend I shared my room with at college was from Reading, and covered by Berkshire County Council. Even though his parents had to pay forty-per cent towards his college education and maintenance, he still got a lot more than me just from his council!

It turned out not to be so bad in the end and I regard myself fortunate to have had a knight in shining armour. Dad stepped in and said he'd help me out financially so that I could buy the essentials I so desperately needed. He did as he promised and each week placed the princely sum of ten pounds into my account.

Although I hadn't noticed it during my childhood, being brought up with little or no cash was the perfect training for college life. I found it easy to budget for the fundamentals – breakfast, horticultural equipment I needed for my course, books, stationery and run my car – on ten pounds a week. I did have to make some economies; like Dad, I'd always put three sugars in my tea and coffee and that had to go. I could only afford to put milk on my cereals, so I got used to black tea and black coffee. But it wasn't all negatives; it didn't take me long to master the art of pacing myself in the student bar or the local pub and managing to last all night on one pint of lager shandy. I found being a cheap date was an attractive prospect, although it would have helped if someone of the opposite sex had found it attractive too.

So, when my car tax came up for renewal I couldn't afford to invest in that as well as breakfast. There was no way that I could survive a hard day of soil science, tomato training and lectures on climatology without a good breakfast inside me, so I had only three options: borrow the money; go without my car, or carry on untaxed.

Going to Dad wasn't an option as he was already supporting me on a weekly basis, and Mum didn't have that sort of spare money, so I did the sensible thing and opted for breakfast, in the belief that education was of far greater importance than the minor misdemeanour of not having road tax. What I hadn't realised was that, should anything happen, my insurance would be invalidated because I didn't have a completely roadworthy car – or any road tax.

That was the reason for the beads of sweat on my brow and my heart having moved up into my mouth. I was sure that the policeman would look at my tax disc and I'd be arrested, hurled into a cell and the key thrown away.

I checked my speed to make sure it was just under 60mph and forged onwards. As I got nearer, he moved to the entrance of the lay-by, where he stood looking statuesque in his magnificently pressed police uniform. His right arm began moving out and upwards and I knew he was about to wave me into the lay-by. Was this the last lay-by I would ever drive into before my lifetime ban for driving with no road tax?

To my astonishment, his arm didn't reach its highest point until I'd passed by. Looking in my rear-view mirror, I saw him wave down the car behind me.

I couldn't speed up to get away before he changed his mind for fear of my suspension giving way and my wheel falling off, although I did feel the need to add a couple of miles per hour to my speed, just in case. When I eventually got to Barnsdale and told my story to Dad, he smiled and reminded me that I'd always been a lucky bugger.

The following morning he asked if I wanted to accompany him into Oakham to do some shopping, which I agreed to as I felt he wanted company during his least favourite task. What I failed to realise was that he'd asked me in a way where I was actually *told* I wanted to go shopping with him and there was no other option.

The 'shopping trip' was in fact to purchase road tax. We parked in the high street and walked the short distance through the marketplace into the main post office. As you would expect on a Saturday morning, the queue was almost to the door, so Dad saved a place while I went to find a V10 road tax application form and filled it in. I joined Dad in the queue, where he stood patiently but rather uncomfortably. I wasn't sure why at the time, but later realised that it was only a couple of years since he'd suffered one of his most embarrassing episodes in that very place.

The last time he'd ventured into the main post office it was for the benefit of his youngest son. Christopher was at college in Bromley and claiming unemployment benefit during the summer holiday – a practice that is no longer possible. However, when he'd filled in the initial claim form the plan was to stay with Dad for the entirety of his holiday. This offer was then withdrawn as Dad's older brother appeared out of the blue, intending to stay for a while. This meant that Christopher's unemployment benefit cheque could only be redeemed in the main Oakham Post Office. Begrudgingly Dad agreed to cashing the benefit cheque for him and then sending on the proceeds. I say begrudgingly because Dad was of the generation where there was a real stigma related to being unemployed, although there was also a certain amount of Rosa-ness in that viewpoint.

The first cheque arrived and he left it until late in the day to cash it, hoping that the post office would be less busy and therefore less chance of anyone thinking it was he that was unemployed. On approaching the counter he felt the need to point out to the young lady sitting behind it that this was not his, he was cashing it on behalf of his youngest son; the Mr C Hamilton printed on the top line. The young lady seemed unmoved by this statement, so he continued. 'It's just that I don't want people to think that it's mine, because I've never been unemployed in my life.' Looking him straight in the eye and without a hint of a smile she just replied, 'Don't worry Mr Hamilton, they'll probably just think you were cashing your pension.' He was only forty-six! It's understandable that he was worried as to what might happen this time.

We shuffled forward. As we neared the front, I wondered what would happen because I had the form but no money to pay for the tax. We arrived at a vacant window and I looked down at my shoes while my benefactor paid the bill.

Returning to the scene of a previous disaster was not something Dad learned from. He'd done the same by returning to Jim for my second car. Datsun cars in the 1980s had a reputation for fantastic engines, but poor bodywork when it came to rust, so it was no surprise that it wasn't worth repairing the suspension of my red Datsun Cherry 100A and scrapping it was the only option.

Dad's next thirty-pound purchase from Jim was a bronze Hillman Imp. This one almost brought him full circle because Cyril had bought him a car to enable him to go to Writtle College, and now Dad was buying me one to keep me there.

Although it wasn't as streamlined as my Datsun and the colour was a bit 'old person' for me, the Imp was a working car and that was the main thing. When I took ownership of it, I did what all car owners do: sat in the driver's seat and tested everything. The steering wheel turned (a good start), the indicators, lights and horn all worked, it had an MOT and the engine fired up when I turned the ignition key.

Dad and Jim looked on as my examination of my new speed machine continued with the outside of the car. All looked in order and the small amount of rust was only to be expected on a car of this age.

Once I'd finished checking the wheels, the next obvious check was of the engine. I lifted the bonnet confidently. There was nothing there, just an empty void where an engine should be. My heart began to race. There must have been an engine somewhere because it fired up when I turned the ignition key, but where was it?

Jim started smiling and giggling, as did Dad once Jim had whispered the reason in his ear. What the hell was happening? I obviously looked completely lost, because Jim suggested that I check the boot. I walked to the rear of my Hillman Imp, opened the boot and, to my complete amazement, found the engine. I hadn't realised that cars could have their engines in the boot rather than under the bonnet.

This workhorse of a car saw me through my last year at college – well almost. It was a carthorse compared to the racehorse Datsun, but it got me to college and back every day and home and back a few times before a technical glitch finished it off completely. This killer blow came when I attempted to fix a blown head gasket. There was no question of taking it to a garage to be fixed. I phoned Dad, who asked Jim for advice as he was much better qualified in the workings of engines than both of us put together.

I needed to know what was causing the Hillman to blow off steam from the radiator generally and how to repair this problem. Jim said the head gasket had blown and needed replacing. According to this engine oracle, this task was made much easier because the engine of a Hillman Imp was made from aluminium so it was lightweight. Apparently a friend and I could lift it out by hand with no need for chains and pulleys. The repair procedure was clearly set out in the Haynes Manual. It sounded easy; so easy that even a complete engine-repairing novice could do it with the relevant Haynes manual in one hand and a spanner in the other.

Finding a friend who was willing to help proved more difficult than I'd imagined, but eventually Darryl agreed. The engine turned out to be twice as heavy as Jim had implied, and therefore twice as heavy as I'd told Darryl. However, we got it out and put it on the floor.

I set about following the instructions in the manual, word for word. It seemed to be a straightforward task that didn't deserve the price the garage had quoted me for the job.

I put back together the parts of the engine I had removed, and all that was left was to lift it back into the boot of my car. Finding another friend (Darryl was not keen on the reverse manoeuvre), we lifted it back in. At this point I should explain that I wear glasses because that goes a long way towards explaining what happened next.

Using the same spanner I had used to loosen all

the nuts, I tightened everything again. I didn't have a torque wrench, which should have been used to tighten the bolts, but I didn't think that mattered – and I didn't have a clue as to what a torque wrench was anyway.

After a week of having to cycle to college and back, the car was fixed and ready. I sat in the driver's seat and prepared myself for the earth-shatteringly exciting moment when I turned the ignition key. I expected the engine to fire up and start to purr…

I turned the key. My goal was fulfilled: water and steam were not pouring out of the radiator. However, even though my goal was achieved, it was very much an own goal. There may have been no steam, but there was no purring either. I turned the key more times than I can remember and although I could hear the starter whirring, the engine refused to fire up.

This was a disaster, not just for me but also for three other students who cadged a lift most mornings. We'd cycled the three and a half miles to college each day and then the three and a half miles back home, and some of them were beginning to struggle.

I thought it might help if I opened the boot and looked at the engine, though I wasn't sure what I was looking for. I went to the troubleshooting section of the Haynes Manual and checked everything they suggested, but nothing seemed to be wrong. Then I hit on the answer – literally. I went back to my toolbox and got out a hammer, hit the engine several times in several different places and returned to the driver's seat.

My confidence that this would solve the problem proved to be misplaced. Still nothing. Had I flooded the engine by turning it over so many times? I'd heard that you could get an engine going by jump-starting it. Maybe I could be towed up the drive of the farm estate where I lived to get it going. I persuaded my friend William to give me a tow with his Citroën 2CV, promising him that the strain to his car would not be fatal. He towed me up the drive and back down it. Still nothing.

I returned to tinkering with the engine, manual in hand, in an attempt to stave off the shame (and enormous expense) of having to admit defeat and tow the car down to the local garage. By now it was getting late and the light was fading. I clearly wasn't going to be able to fix it and the only course of action was the mechanic and his garage down the road.

I tentatively phoned the 'Bank of Dad'. He also knew that was the only choice, so after college on Monday William and I towed the car to the local garage and left it there for them to look at. The mechanic said it would be ready by Wednesday afternoon. I told him that I'd had a little tinker with the engine, but couldn't find the problem. Apparently he looked concerned, but I was now thinking about other things and didn't notice.

Midday on Wednesday arrived and I got into my taxi (also known as William and his 2CV) and went to the garage. I was in such a good mood because I would soon be mobile again, and I was sure I'd be congratulated on my mechanical expertise in almost getting the job done.

At the garage, I rang the bell on the reception counter. Several rings later, the mechanic finally appeared. I was beaming and ready for the praise I was about to get; he started to beam back then moved his head from side to side. I had an inkling that this might not be a good sign.

I have to give him credit for making a valiant attempt not to make me look a complete idiot while explaining the problem, but he was not successful.

Now, if I'd have been in his position I'd have probably eased into the reasons gently and gradually built up to the finale. He didn't. He went straight for the jugular and asked which idiot hadn't put the timing chain back in the correct place when putting the engine back together.

The timing chain. I didn't actually remember that being mentioned in the manual. I'd never heard of a timing chain before and didn't know its function. I had placed what looked like a short bicycle chain back on the cog it had been on before but, as I was to find out, this wasn't the proper way. Apparently I didn't put the same links of the chain over the same spikes on the cog that they'd been on when it was removed. I started to think that maybe this could be a problem as he continued to rub it in.

This meant that when I was towed up and down the drive the chain turned on the cog, bringing the valves out into each cylinder chamber just as the engine pistons were coming to the top of their cycle. Even a non-mechanically minded person like myself realised that this was not a good thing. Apparently the valves are supposed to come out into the cylinders when each piston is at its *lowest* point in the cylinder, or something like that.

The pistons had hit the valves and bent them all, as well as damaging the inside of the cylinders in the process. The mechanic pointed out that he'd never seen valves bent quite so badly in all his time in the trade. Basically my car was a write-off because the cost of a reconditioned engine was twice the value of the car once the engine had been fitted.

My short trip back home with William and his 2CV wasn't a chatty one. I was devastated at annihilating my Hillman Imp, and William was reeling at the shock of finding out he was now the only student on the farm estate with a car.

When I got home, I decided to revisit the Haynes Manual. If the timing chain wasn't mentioned, could I get them to replace the car because they'd misinformed me? I was certain there was no mention of it when I'd meticulously read the pages as I repaired the Imp.

I reread the section about replacing the head gasket and there was no mention of the timing chain. Then I turned over the page. Now, as I said before, I need glasses... It turns out that there was a beautifully written section all about the timing chain; it even stated, in bold letters, the need to return the chain to its exact position. It takes an element of skill and poor eyesight to completely miss not just one section of an instruction manual, but the most important section of an instruction manual.

After I left college and prior to starting work, it was back to Dad. He invested in an Alfa Romeo Alfasud to get me mobile. Again he bought a car from Jim for a meagre amount. You really would have thought he'd learned his lesson by now, but he was obviously trying to gently ease me to the point where I'd consider buying my own, better vehicle.

I got into the car to see how it felt and examine the controls. Once behind the wheel, I was overcome with a feeling that I'd never had before. I felt cool, I felt suave, and I felt sophisticated. I had a sports car – not your archetypal sports car like a Porsche, Jaguar or an Aston Martin, but sporty enough for a horticulturalist. I sat for a while and soaked it all in, certain that this moment was unlikely to ever happen again.

If the Datsun went like a rocket, this car went like a turbocharged rocket. I loved it. However, my love affair with the car, my coolness, suaveness and sophistication were short-lived.

The fateful day was a Sunday in September, on my journey back home from a visit to Mum in Kettering. I'd only travelled about ten minutes, taking the scenic route back to my digs in Norfolk and tootling along a lovely country road, when suddenly there was a really loud grinding noise from under the left-hand side of the bonnet. Not again! I was approaching Grafton

Underwood where it was safe to stop but the noise got louder, so I took an executive decision and pulled into the next field gateway. After lifting the bonnet and spending a considerable time looking for a problem, my vastly inexperienced mechanical brain decided that it wasn't under there, so I began to check the exterior.

It couldn't be the suspension again, could it? Although a small stone trapped between a brake pad and the braking disc had made a similar noise once before and it had been an easy job to fix. Like all good horticulturalists, I'd had my gardening knife in my pocket, so it had been easy to flick it out and go on my way.

There was no traffic, so I decided to check the roadside wheels first. I couldn't see any stones on either the front or back wheels, so I moved round to the other side. It was then that I noticed the front wheel seemed to be pushed into the back of the wheel arch. I tried to move it but it wouldn't budge, so I got back into the car, started it up and moved fractionally backwards. Out I hopped, hoping that the wheel wasn't now in the front of the wheel arch but, lo and behold, there it was.

I decided that the car wasn't drivable, so I walked to a public phone box in Grafton Underwood to call my friend Tony. He picked me up and took me back to Mum's.

When the recovery chap dropped my car at the Alfa Romeo workshop in Kettering, I'd arranged to collect it on the following Saturday morning. Tony kindly offered to loan me his Ford Cortina so that I could get to my place of work in Norfolk. At the end of my working week I rang to check it was ready, but there was no reply. I assumed the mechanics were busy and tootled down to the garage anyway. When I arrived, to my horror I saw the burnt-out remains of what had been the workshop.

I scanned the small number of fire-damaged cars standing at the edge of the site, but mine wasn't there. Suddenly I was whisked back to the woodwork workshop blaze at school and the mental scarring caused by the totally unnecessary burning of my wall cabinet. The only difference in this case was that the fire hadn't been started by a disgruntled customer but by the owner himself!

Worse was to come. Dad had set me up initially with my insurance and I'd carried this on with all my subsequent vehicles. He was clear when he paid for it that if I damaged the car I would pay for the repairs. His theory was that this would make me drive more carefully. Consequently I was insured on a third-party only basis, primarily because nobody with any sense would ever consider stealing my cars. Neither of us had considered the fire element of insurance. There was no payout for my burnt-out shell of a car – not that it was worth much in the first place.

Dad rarely missed an opportunity and he saw opportunity in my loss. Somehow this automotive and personal disaster became the chance to shed responsibility.

Before the ash had even settled he stated that, as I had left college and was in full-time employment, his responsibility for providing my transport had come to an end. This came as a bit of a shock but before long I was on the phone to my bank to arrange an interview to discuss a loan. Dad had nudged me into taking on my own responsibilities without my even noticing.

A week later I was the proud owner of my very own, one-year-old, white Ford Fiesta.

Chapter 20

Dad's sense of responsibility towards his children rose and sank depending on the occasion. He was adept at ducking, but when he felt strongly about something he was just as good at standing up and being counted.

Mum took care of my annual hospital trips because Dad was always busy at work, but there's no question that he could have taken time off at least once to take me. However, the fact is that he didn't like hospitals so he ducked the responsibility. Although his duty to educate me in the arts of discussion, consultation and striking a deal instead of punching your teacher in his goolies was one he couldn't avoid. Where my education was concerned, he always did whatever he could, whenever he could.

During the first few weeks of my disastrous A-level studies, Dad reminded me more than once that I should choose a horticultural college as soon as possible so that I could reserve a place. One lunchtime we were sitting in his kitchen eating lunch whilst I jotted down the names of colleges as Dad reeled them off. Some I'd heard of before, but others were incomprehensible as he burbled then out through a mouth full of bread and goat's cheese. In hindsight, this was probably not the best time to carry out this operation as eating took priority. He then sent me away to find out the addresses for each college and to send off for prospectuses.

A couple of weeks later our coffee table was straining under the weight of many glossy horticultural college brochures. By the time I saw Dad again I'd read them all and discounted about half, with the remainder still 'possible'. There were three definite favourites: Pershore College, Writtle Agricultural College and Wye College.

Dad had already started to drop subtle hints about how good Writtle College was, which was no surprise as this was the college he'd attended. His interest in my obtaining these prospectuses was well-timed (planned!) because a few weeks later there was a trade show at the NEC in Birmingham called The British Growers Look Ahead (BGLA). This was THE show to go to because hundreds of horticultural companies as well as all of the horticultural colleges worth their salt would be exhibiting. Dad went every year and he suggested that I should accompany him; he would make sure that we visited every college stand. By the end of the day, I'd have a much clearer idea which college would give me the best training. That seemed pretty straightforward.

When we arrived at the NEC, the BGLA was spread over several massive halls. I wasn't sure how we were going to find all the colleges unless they were all in one section. They weren't, but that wasn't a problem because

Dad had a map, together with a list of the people and businesses he needed to see. His plan was that I could visit the college stands as we passed them.

It was supposedly a coincidence that the first stand we came across was for Writtle Agricultural College. Dad seemed very surprised to see it so quickly into our jaunt round; he really wasn't a great actor, so it's fortunate he had a natural ability at presenting on television when the time came.

What Dad didn't know was that the stand was being manned by the only lecturer left at Writtle who had taught him: Ian Lambert, who lectured on glasshouse crops. This was the twilight of Mr Lambert's lecturing years, but he still had great presence and could control any situation.

Dad recognised him immediately, and they had a short period of reminiscing and catching up. Then Dad introduced me to his old teacher, who was very keen to hear about my prospective career path and even keener when I told him it was to be horticulture. Dad was very keen also – keen to make sure I said all the right things in all the right places. Gradually he started to do all the talking.

Mr Lambert, as I was to discover later, was not the sort of lecturer who tolerated this kind of behaviour. Dad had obviously forgotten that. Finally Mr Lambert turned to Dad, who was in the middle of replying to a question that had been directed at me, and firmly but politely asked him to stop talking and go and sit down.

He pointed to a chair in the corner of the stand, well away from where we – or anyone else – were standing. Dad shuffled off like a naughty schoolboy while I had a long chat with Mr Lambert. I discovered all I needed to know about the college and firmly fixed Writtle at the top of my list.

Once Mr Lambert had said all he needed to say, we shook hands. He summoned Dad from his seat in the 'naughty corner' and we all said our goodbyes. I was fired up and ready to soak up all the information on offer from the other colleges exhibiting at the show.

I have subsequently been to the BGLA many, many times and I have no idea how Dad did it, but he managed to steer us to all the stands he needed to visit without ever passing another college stand. Had he spent an evening at home plotting his route?

Dad knew the quality of the education offered at Writtle and was keen for me to have the horticultural training he'd had. It was a masterful stroke, though one he never admitted to, and after such a good sell by Mr Lambert, it was Writtle College for me.

When my interview for Writtle came through, I was surprised that Dad leapt in with an offer to be my taxi service. I was eighteen and couldn't drive, so his offer came as a blessing as the train journey would have been complicated. When the time came, however, he had to pull out due to a last-minute filming commitment, but he had organised a substitute who was more than happy to take me. He had recruited 'The Dream Team' – Rosa and Cyril.

Fortunately, the two poodles (Pom-Pom and Poppet) who'd been the bane of our younger lives had passed to the great poodle heaven in the sky. To me it seemed like these two dogs had lived to at least 347, not in dog years but in human years. Their age meant they had very bad dog halitosis and a very bad wind problem. As children we would occupy the back seat with the poodles, so it was a relief when they were no longer with us.

The car wasn't dog-free for long. The new member of their family was a toy Yorkshire terrier called Titch. Fortunately for me, he was young with excellent control over his digestive system and good dental hygiene. The car was a Renault and, as was the norm back then, the man drove when they travelled together. I was collected from Kettering and took up my position on the back seat with Titch. I have to say that our conversation wasn't very exciting but I suppose Titch was from a different generation to me.

We'd just left Kettering when there was a disagreement between my driver and navigator. Cyril might be behind the steering wheel, but it seemed it was Rosa who was actually in control of the driving. After a brief exchange, she got her way and we set off down the A6.

Cyril's driving wasn't as good as I'd expected, bearing in mind he'd spent about half of his working life travelling the length and breadth of the UK. It had seemed much better when I was little, but then I had no concept of fear at that age.

The A6 has never been a slow road and when the driver of your vehicle starts to drift over the centre line and then back towards the verge, it's rather nerve-wracking for the rear-seat passenger. Any concerns I had the first time it happened doubled at the second deviation, and tripled at the third one. By the fourth, I was having palpitations. I started hoping that something would go wrong with the car and curtail our journey. I was so frightened that I was prepared to forego my interview rather than see my life end.

According to some people, if you channel your thoughts and focus on one thing, that thing will happen. I didn't believe that – but then, without warning, smoke or steam started to pour out from under the bonnet. We could see a petrol station visible in the distance and Cyril, under clear instruction, pulled onto the forecourt. I was delighted and began to look forward to our return journey on the back of a recovery vehicle.

To Cyril and Rosa's relief, the garage was also a repair workshop. Needless to say, I was gutted when a mechanic appeared, spanner in hand. He lifted the bonnet and started his inspection. I knew that I shouldn't wish ill on a close relative, but I hoped that the engine was completely wrecked.

While the car was being assessed, Grandma Rosa saw an opportunity. I was sure she knew that I had caused the problem with my new-found mind power and she needed me out of the way. She asked if I could walk Titch up and down the garage forecourt so he could stretch his legs. I don't know why this was necessary; his legs were so short that just getting out of the car and back in would have stretched them beyond recognition.

My worry about whether the mechanic was going to fix the engine disappeared very quickly as I realised that we were only ten miles from Kettering. There was no way I was going to risk being seen by anyone I knew walking up and down on the A6 with this dog. I didn't have any street credibility to worry about, but I didn't want to ruin the chance of future street credibility by being spotted.

I opted for the 'having to go to the toilet' trick. I knew I'd have to wait there until the mechanic had finished. Rosa knocked on the door a couple of times to check I was all right. I took a chance and emerged a good twenty minutes later to find that the diagnosis was that the thermostat in the Renault had stayed shut. This was a common problem on this make of car but it could only be repaired by a Renault garage. In an extraordinary stroke of good fortune, the garage we were at wasn't a Renault garage so couldn't help.

I couldn't believe my luck. My grandparents were very apologetic, with Cyril even suggesting risking the rest of the journey, but I put on a brave face and said I was sure the college would understand and I could rearrange the interview. Inside I was jumping with joy.

When the next interview came around, Dad was again to be the volunteer driver and this time nothing got in the way. We had a very pleasant and uneventful trip down to Essex, with Dad's inbuilt satnav finding the college at the first attempt. Apparently not much had changed in the twenty-five years since he'd attended.

Once we'd parked outside the main college building, I made Dad sit in the car. I was determined that if I was going to be offered a place then I was going to do it on my own, with no interference from a well-known horticulturalist and ex-Writtle student.

Dad was fine with that and, for once, did as he was told. He only left the car to have a mooch round to see how things had changed since his day. The only drawback was the Spanish Inquisition on the way home until I'd recounted exactly what had been said, word for word. He was confident I'd done enough to be accepted; he didn't say so, but he immediately started to give me advice on what I should do when I started there.

I listened half-heartedly, as some of Dad's advice wasn't particularly great. The Tarzan tree episode was a fine example. At the age of seven you can get very excited by the thought of a tree swing, especially when it's one your Dad used to swing on as a child. I was also a great fan of Tarzan on the television, and saw myself very much as a younger Ron Ely – I was too good looking to be a younger Johnny Weissmuller.

The three of us jumped into the back seat of the car and were driven into the countryside. It was only about a mile out of Broxbourne, but I thought I was on a jungle expedition.

It was always going to take much longer than expected

to get anywhere in the Austin Morris, but eventually we arrived and parked on a quiet, narrow country road. As an explorer, you know that your day's going to be an exciting one when your first task is to negotiate a five-bar gate. Being the middle son, I got the middle bit of the gate with the cross members; it felt like mountaineering up a sheer rock face covered in mosses and ferns, looking for footholds that would take my weight without creating a major rockfall. Not that I'd ever been mountaineering, or even hillwalking, but I had seen enough of Ron climbing rock faces and trees to be fully tutored in the skill. The mountain peaked sooner than expected and the descent down the north face was so rapid that I was pleased to get my feet firmly on terra firma.

Surveying the savannah in front of me, I saw a large expanse of long, green grass (also known as a field) with a treelike object visible in the distance. As we approached I could see that this object was indeed a tree: one with no bark on it, and horizontal. Having been promised tree climbing and swinging, this really wasn't what we were expecting. Dad looked confused; he said that the last time he'd seen this tree it was upright, covered in bark and clothed in leaves with a rope dangling from it. It turned out that this was some twenty years earlier.

Dad took a moment to think and concluded that the Tarzan tree had been struck by lightning, which had not only brought it down but also burnt off the bark. He wasn't daft; he knew the thought of lightning and fire would be exciting to his children, and it was.

We followed his suggestion of climbing the tree in a horizontal fashion. Ron Ely had leapt over a fallen tree while escaping the attentions of a lion just the week before, so I felt very much at home. As swinging was now impossible, Dad promised a trip to the stream that ran along the far edge of the field. The prospect of water, climbing overhanging trees, stream leaping and spotting sticklebacks was overwhelming, and certainly of more interest than clambering over a fallen tree. In the world of Tarzan, I suppose it's hard to imagine sticklebacks being a decent substitute for a river full of crocodiles, but they are when you're a desperate seven-year-old. Off we set.

Dad was at his best when thinking on his feet, so planning was not something that he indulged in too often. In this case, some planning might have been beneficial. We were too busy telling each other what we would do when we got to the stream to notice that there was another inhabitant in the field and we were gradually approaching him.

Suddenly I was distracted by something that I glimpsed out of the corner of my eye. I glanced to my right and noticed a rather large, muscular black body attached to four sturdy black legs. My eyes moved slowly along the rippling body and spotted large and damp flared nostrils, through which was a silver-coloured ring. Moving past the staring eyes, I saw two very large and very pointed horns. At this point I tugged Dad's arm and asked why the bull, standing menacingly in the corner of the field, was staring at us.

I wasn't frightened often, but the only images I had seen of bulls up to then had been of short-tempered, vicious animals whose intent was to spear you with their fearsome-looking horns.

Being the adult in the pack, Dad's advice at this point was critical, and I was sure he would give the desperate situation the consideration it deserved. He did – and shouted 'RUN'.

I didn't have to be told twice. I was off. In fact, we were all off. We turned and ran as if our lives depended on it. My little legs were whirring like the propellers on a Spitfire. All thoughts of mimicking Ron Ely's escape from Simba across the African savannah disappeared as fear for my life took over. Ron never looked as panicked as I felt in that moment.

I passed the Tarzan tree and the five-bar gate came into view. All of a sudden this tall figure streaked past me: it was Dad going at full pace. He reached the gate first and hurdled it in one go; irritatingly, he was far better than I had been in my 100-metre school hurdle race.

He turned and shouted at us from the safety of the other side of the gate, 'Speed up, speed up!' with an occasional, 'He's catching up with you!' thrown in for good measure. For once I was delighted that I was bow-legged because this created less drag and more speed as the air flew unobstructed through the gaping hole between my legs. I finally reached the gate and all thoughts of getting over it as quickly as possible overrode my earlier sheer-cliff-face Tarzan fantasy.

This time I scaled the gate with just one foot on the second horizontal bar. I landed hands first and then went into a forward roll, finishing prostrate on the damp, grassy verge. There was no time to take breath, however, because the vicious bull could come crashing through the gate at any moment.

Dad was already in the car and we piled in after him. As we pulled away, I looked to see how close we'd come to death and if the bull had made it to the gate. He wasn't there and there was no sign of him. As we passed a gap in the hedge, I saw him in the same place where I'd first spotted him. His head was bent, damp nostrils embedded in the long grass and his bottom jaw moving from side to side as he munched on the grass, obviously without a care in the world.

There was no question that, having dispensed his rather hasty advice, Dad just had to see it through.

A month after my college interview, a letter arrived from Writtle College to say that I'd been accepted onto the Commercial Horticulture OND Sandwich Course. I was so excited: this was the start of my life in horticulture and a great adventure. I was so excited, that I couldn't phone Dad; instead I leapt on my moped and whizzed over to Barnsdale, acceptance letter firmly gripped in my hand.

I'd never seen such a grin on Dad's face as the one that

appeared as he read the letter. He wasn't an emotional person, but it was clear that he was pleased and very proud.

Now I was ready for the 'what you need to know before you go to college' advice. However, being a practical person and having read the bit that said I needed to do a year's work experience in the industry before going to college, he decided that it wasn't time for advice. Instead, he went all Spanish on me again and the brutal inquisition started. Had I thought about where I'd like to work? What area of horticulture did I want to try? Had I contacted anyone, etc., etc. I'd only received the letter an hour and a half ago, so how he thought I'd done any of this I don't know. What I do know was that Dad was determined I wouldn't ruin my chances of getting into Writtle.

Eventually, when the excited questioning subsided, the one thing he did make absolutely clear was that I couldn't do my year's work experience at Barnsdale. According to Dad, it wouldn't look good if I did my work experience with a family member. That meant no work for *Garden News* or *Practical Gardening*, even though he was still the editor of the latter. I understood his reasoning, although I would have taken any opportunity to work with him. He was my idol and I wanted to be as close to him as possible for as long as possible.

Over the next few days, it dawned on me that he hadn't been totally adverse to working with his family, not being slow to take up my offers of free help when he moved into Barnsdale, or on many other occasions. I'd even been recruited to appear on the front cover of *Practical Gardening*, presumably because of my extensive modelling experience. That was for an issue on lawn care, so I was posed as if I was pushing a mower across the front lawn of his cottage. I had done as I was told and turned up in a pair of clean jeans, a decent shirt and a pair of wellies. The problem was that the shirt, which I'd chosen from my extensive collection of two shirts, was deemed not colourful enough.

I was in a fairly traumatised state when I arrived, having decided to ride my moped the twenty-five miles from home in my wellies. That made gear-changing somewhat hazardous, although I was kitted out for any large puddles. Rod Sloane, the EMAP photographer extraordinaire, had brought a bright-red shirt with him and I grudgingly put it on. After all, I reminded myself, when it came to modelling I was a professional.

When the magazine was published, it was the lawnmower and not the bright red shirt that took centre stage on the cover. That proved Rod knew his stuff, because all the colours on the front cover blended perfectly. This issue turned out to be really popular with the gardening public and sold far more copies than usual. As I said to Dad, this was obviously because of the incredibly attractive cover.

Two weeks after publication, Dad received a phone call from John Kenyon. Dad hadn't heard of him because John Kenyon wasn't a horticulturalist – he was a television producer. And he wasn't just any television producer; he was the producer of BBC 2's *Gardeners' World*. Dad didn't have a television but knew of the programme and its presenters, most of whom he'd met at journalism events, but he didn't know any of the team that made the programme.

John phoned to ask if Dad would like to appear as a gardening expert and help one of the presenters on the following week's programme. He was keen to feature Dad as he was a well-known horticulturalist, being the editor of the country's top-selling gardening magazine. Dad agreed to appear. Can I just mention that at no point did Dad give my front-cover appearance the credit it deserved for helping to launch his new career?

He tootled off to the Pebble Mill Studios in Birmingham, did his bit, then tootled back to his cottage in Rutland. He was pleased with his day, feeling that he'd made a good contribution to the programme. However, John was of a different opinion. He'd seen something, something he'd not seen before in any presenter he'd worked with on *Gardeners' World*. He saw great potential, and he knew that together he and Geoff Hamilton could change television gardening forever. Was he right? Was this going to be the start of the best gardening programme ever, fronted by the best television gardener ever?

Lightning Source UK Ltd.
Milton Keynes UK
UKHW011816300322
400845UK00001B/11

9 781914 083426